Waterstones
8·99

CUT 'N' MIX

CULTURE, IDENTITY
AND CARIBBEAN MUSIC

Dick Hebdige

A Comedia book
published by Routledge
London and New York

A Comedia book
First published in 1987 by
Methuen & Co. Ltd

Reprinted 1990, 1993 by Routledge
11 New Fetter Lane, London EC4P 4EE
29 West 35th Street, New York NY 10001

© 1987 Dick Hebdige

Printed in Great Britain by Unwin Brothers Ltd, The Gresham Press,
Old Woking, Surrey.
Typeset by Photosetting, 6 Foundry House, Stars Lane, Yeovil,
Somerset.

British Library Cataloguing in Publication Data
Hebdige, Dick
    Cut 'n' Mix: Culture, identity and Caribbean music.
    1. Music — Caribbean area
    I. Title
781.7'09182'1   ML3565

ISBN 0 415 05875 9 (Paperback)

Cover Design by Andy Dark

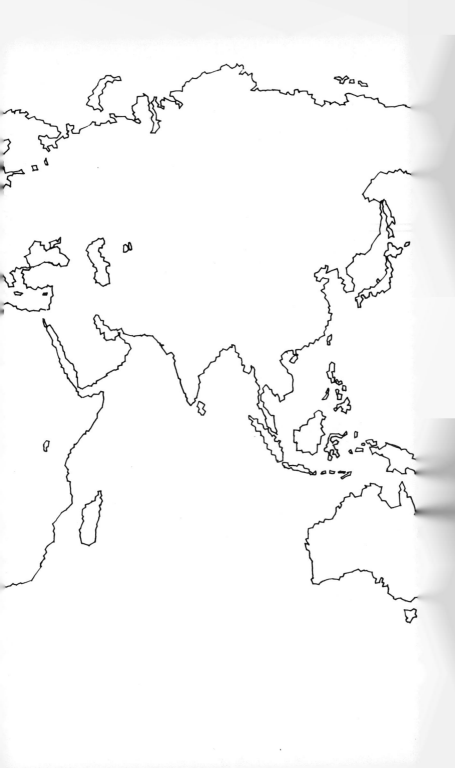

Acknowledgements

In his book *There Ain't No Black In The Union Jack* (Hutchinson, forthcoming), Paul Gilroy has suggested that music functions within the culture of the black diaspora as an alternative public sphere. Sometimes a reggae toast or a soul rap might consist of little more than a list of names or titles. Naming can be in and of itself an act of invocation, conferring power and/or grace upon the namer: the names can carry power in themselves. The titles bestowed on Haile Selassie in a Rastafarian chant or a reggae toast or on James Brown or Aretha Franklin in a soul or MC rap testify to this power. More importantly in this context, the namer pays tribute in the "name check" to the community from which (s)he has sprung and without which (s)he would be unable to survive. The speaker or singer's individual voice is drowned beneath the sea of names which it summons up around itself.

There are many people without whom this book could not have been written. I would like to thank Albert on the door, Bonk, Mikey, Steve Gibbons, Pete King, Martin and Simon Fuller, Norrie Davis, Paul, Vron and Marcus, Greg, Rosa and David, Sam Rosenberg, Iain Chambers, Roy Bailey, Geoff H, Su Fawcett, my mother and father, Charlie Luck, Griff, Ken Brown, Clinton, Alan Bayes, Larry Grossberg, Red Rum, Clare, Patrick and Edward, Van Cagle, Dave Darby, Polly M, Prudence, Vic Lockwood, Maggie and Trevor, Mo, Peta Legat, Serafina, Steve Bonnett, Richard Madgwick, Paul Swinson, Jessica Lucy Pickard, Jordi Rippoles, Winston at the Three Crowns, Kathy K, and the Golden Eagle (the one that flew away).

I would also like to thank all the singers, musicians, producers, engineers, djs and microphone artists who make the music this book is about. A special word of thanks to: The Skatalites, James Brown, Toots and the Maytals, Ranking Ann, Bob Marley and the Wailers, Big Youth, Jerry Dammers and the Specials with Rico, Don Drummond, Grandmaster Flash and the Furious Five, Peggy Lee, Sly and the Family Stone, Etta James, Miles Davis, Afrika Bambaata, the Soul Sonic Force and the Zulu Nation, Howling Wolf, Smokey Robinson and the Miracles, Shirley Brown, Gene Vincent, Gregory Isaacs, Dion, Exuma, John Coltrane, Dennis Brown and

Aswad, Niney, Barbara Jones, I Roy, Elvis Presley, Lee "Scratch" Perry, Joe Gibbs, Esther Phillips, Mickey and Sylvia, Tina and Ike, The Angels, Gram Parsons, Shirley Ellis, Jimmy Hendrix, Sam Cooke, Eek a Mouse, Billie Holliday, Dinah Washington, Booker T and the MGs, Patsy Cline, Pharoah Saunders, Bo Diddley, Malcolm McLaren, John Lydon, Ben E King, The Fatback Band, The JBs, Fela Kuti, U Roy, Roland Kirk, The Yardbirds, Planxty, The Ohio Players, Linton Johnson, The Ronettes, Basil Gabbidon, UB40, Johann Sebastian Bach, Billy Fury, Otis Redding, Hank Williams, Executor, Mighty Sparrow, Black Stalin, Prince Buster, Count Ossie, Dennis Bovell and Steel Pulse.

I should like to thank all the writers, radio and music business personnel whose work I have used, quoted or otherwise borrowed from: Dotun Adebayo, Verena Reckford, Andrew Carr, J L Collier, Robert Elms, Carl Gayle, Sheryl Garratt, Paul Gilroy (again), Tony Harrison, Steven Hager, Steven Harvey, John Hind and Stephen Mosco, Simon Jones, Junior Lincoln, Amanda Lipman, Vic Lockwood, Jeremy Marre and Hannah Charlton, Colin McGlashan, Miss P, Mr Fresh and the Supreme Rockers, George Oban, Joe Owens, J Plummer, Penny Reel, Vivien Goldman, David Simmons and David Toop.

I should especially like to thank Albert Goldman for the *Elvis* extracts in the Pre-Mix, Alex Haley for the extract from *Roots* in Chapter One, Garry Wills for the extract from "Martin Luther King is still on the case" in Chapter Five, Stephen Davis and Chris May for all their work on music – it is always well researched, well written and of a consistently high standard – and I've drawn a great deal on the articles Chris May wrote for *Black Music* on reggae in the 1970s and on Stephen Davis' two books on reggae music – *Reggae Bloodlines* and *Reggae International*. Thanks, too, to Ed Lee for doing a fine edit on the first version of the Original Cut. And thanks, finally, to Dave Morley of Comedia for his patience, tact and resourcefulness in dealing with a succession of impossible requests, for the imagination and hard work he has brought to bear on this project. And to Andy Dark for designing the visual mix.

A special word of thanks to Patrick Ward for the laughs and for the poetry; to Mike Stanhope for sounds and brotherhood; to Mike Horseman for being Major Spar, Vinyl King and The Music Man of the Midlands; and to Paul Gilroy for taking so much time and care to answer what must have seemed to him like elementary questions. Without these last four, I wouldn't have been able to undertake, let alone complete, this project. Finally thanks to Amstrad who have brought William Burroughs to the High Street by bringing cut 'n' mix technology to bear upon the word.

A note on the title of this book

The title of this book may appear misleading. The words "cut" and "mix" have particular connotations within popular music and the record industry. They refer to editing procedures. And when placed together they tend to summon up the image of a sound engineer working at an editing desk or a hip hop dj scratching sounds together at a turntable. Both these figures will be invoked in what follows, but this is not what the book is principally about. Instead what I was interested in when I was writing this book is the relationship between Caribbean music and cultural identity. I have tried to conceive that relationship in dynamic terms. Rather than tracing back the roots of contemporary forms of Caribbean music to their source, I've tried to show how the roots themselves are in a state of constant flux and change. The roots don't stay in one place. They change shape. They change colour. And they grow. There is no such thing as a pure point of origin, least of all in something as slippery as music, but that doesn't mean there isn't history. I hope the two notes clarify – if nothing else – the *intention* that motivated the pages that follow.

Cut 'n' mix

Cut 'n' mix is the music and the style of the 1980s just as rock 'n' roll and rhythm 'n' blues formed the bedrock for the musics and the styles that have made such an impact on our culture since the 1950s. This book doesn't try to tell the whole story because the *whole* story can't be told. The story of cut 'n' mix is too jumbled up and unpredictable to be captured in a book. And every day new connections are being made that create potentialities which are unimagined here. The journey from African drums to the Roland TR 808 drum machine, or from the Nigerian "griots" to UB40 and Ranking Ann doesn't run in straight lines like a sentence on a page. It circles back upon itself at every opportunity. And nobody can catch a sound on paper because a sound melts into air as soon as it's made. If I've learnt one lesson from this project it's that everybody writes in time.

Culture, Identity and Caribbean music

African, Afro-American and Caribbean music is based on quite different principles from the European classical tradition. The collective voice is given precedence over the individual voice of the artist or the composer. Rhythm and percussion play a much more central role. In the end, there is a link in these non-European musics with public life, with speech, with the textures and the grain of the living human voice. And these links are maintained first and last through drumming. Where there is drumming there is dancing. At the end we always find the human body writhing like a fish on the line and the hook of the rhythm. This book is about some of those rhythms and the links that can be made between rhythm and speech, between cultures, histories and identities.

Pre-mix: version to version

"U Roy takes the microphone and passes it to Big Youth, who takes it up and gives it to General Echo. Echo chats a verse or two and hands the mike to Papa Michigan and General Smiley, The Lone Ranger, Philip Levi and Smiley Culture... From version to version, from verse to verse."

(Dotun Adebayo)

"As a young man who had heard a vast amount of music but who had no greater musical resources than his vocal chords, his rhythm guitar and his tiny two-piece semipro 'band', Elvis Presley found himself in the familiar position of the musically inspired, musically initiated, but musically deprived all over the world. His solution to his problem was the classic solution... he made himself into a one-man band."

(Albert Goldman)[1]

One of the most important words in reggae is "version". Sometimes a reggae record is released and literally hundreds of different versions of the same rhythm or melody will follow in its wake. Every time a version is released, the original tune will be slightly modified. A musician will play a different solo on a different instrument, use a different tempo, key or chord sequence. A singer will place the emphasis on different words or will add new ones. A record producer will use a different arrangement. An engineer will stretch the sounds into different shapes, add sound effects, take out notes and chords or add new ones, creating empty spaces by shuffling the sequence of sounds into new patterns. To give just one example: Wayne Smith made a record called *Under Mi Sleng Teeng*. It has been estimated that by October, 1985, no less than 239 versions of this tune had been made.

"Versioning" is at the heart not only of reggae but of *all* Afro-American and Caribbean musics: jazz, blues, rap, r&b, reggae, calypso, soca, salsa, Afro-Cuban and so on. With the advent of twelve-inch discs in the late 1970s, the same principle has been extended to black American soul. Now it's normal on a twelve-inch to get several different versions of the same number: an *original cut*, a *dub* version where the rhythm is shaken out and played with, and a *club mix* where it is remixed again in still another version. And the at the beginning of rock 'n' roll, in Elvis Presley's vocal style. In his book *Elvis*, the American critic Albert Goldman shows how Presley did his own parodic versions of other artists' songs and singing styles:

> "The secret of Elvis' art lay not in an act of substantive creation but in a recasting of one traditional style in terms of another. To make such a transposition, you have to be stylistically sophisticated. You have to see all the familiar styles lying before you like so many spots of colour on a painter's palette. Such sophistication would have taken many years to develop in the premedia world of popular music. Once, however, every American child started growing up with unlimited access to every kind of music provided by radio, any boy with a good ear and the necessary talent could get hip fast. [And] Elvis Presley was from his earliest years a marvellous mimic..."[2]

To say that Elvis was a mimic is not to diminish his talent or his achievement. The fact that he could do a perfect imitation of Dean Martin crooning a Neapolitan love song or Arthur Crudup shouting out a gutsy blues or Hank Williams whining his way through some tortured cowboy lament didn't stop him making his own style by blending all the other styles together. He could borrow different voices, different styles at different times and in the process he created something of his own.

> "During his Sun years, he used his talent to create a music that was essentially playful and parodistic. In approaching pop song in this spirit, he established the basic aesthetic for rock 'n' roll. Rock is not, as is always said, simply an amalgam of blues, country, pop, etc. This is to define it by its sources and substances instead of its soul. The music's essence lies in its attitude. This attitude first comes to expression in Elvis, then in Little Richard and then in the Beatles, to name the greatest performers in the tradition. All of these singers are at bottom parodists ... What's more, the degree of sophistication, allusion and fantasy in their work may vary greatly from the purely instinctive sass of Little Richard to the much more calculated 'styling' of Elvis to the sometimes brilliantly resourceful travesties of John Lennon, which shade into the bizarre but compelling juxtapositions of surrealism. The important thing is to recognise that the root of rock is in the put-on and the take-off, the characteristic fusion of enthusiasm and mockery that was

almost universal in the pop culture of the fifties: a slant on things that you find as much in *Mad* or the routines of Sid Caesar or the comic pornography of Terry Southern as you do in the funny songs of Leiber and Stoller or the funny singing of Elvis Presley."[3]

In other words, Elvis did his own "version" of Dean Martin, Arthur Crudup, Hank Williams, just as I am doing *my* own version of what Albert Goldman was doing in the passages I've just quoted. And just as Elvis *used* the voices and the vocal styles of the other singers, so I have borrowed Albert Goldman's voice and style to say something about "versioning". That's what a quotation in a book or on record is. It's an invocation of someone else's voice to help you say what you want to say. In order to *e*-voke you have to be able to *in*-voke. And every time the other voice is borrowed in this way, it is turned away slightly from what it was the original author or singer or musician thought they were saying, singing, playing. When I quote Albert Goldman's words, it doesn't necessarily mean I agree with every word he wrote in *Elvis*. For instance, I don't think that Little Richard is any more "purely instinctive" in his work than John Lennon was. And in their original context these comments on Elvis' early vocal style – comments which are in my opinion highly perceptive – are intended to be damning. Albert Goldman thinks that Elvis was such a good mimic that he became a "commercial copycat". I just think that the early Elvis was a great vocal stylist and that Albert Goldman provides us here with one key to his greatness. That's the beauty of quotation. The original version takes on a new life and a new meaning in a fresh context. Just like a rhythm or a melody which is brought in from another source in a record or in the live performance of a piece of music. They're just different *kinds* of quotation. And that's the beauty, too, of versioning. It's a democratic principle because it implies that no one has the final say. Everybody has a chance to make a contribution. And no one's version is treated as Holy Writ.

In what I take to be the spirit of the "version", I have made copious use of quotations in this book. There is in a sense nothing "original" about what I have to say at all. Everything I know about Caribbean music I've learned from listening to it on record and tape, by going to see it played and performed, by talking to other people or by reading about it. I've never been to the Caribbean. The Acknowledgements at the front of this book are not merely a nod to a writerly convention. My version owes a great deal to other people and to other people's versions.

This book is in a sense three separate books or three tracks on a single rhythm. It consists of three versions on the theme of culture, identity and Caribbean music written from different perspectives at different times. The first version – what I've called the "Original Cut" was written in 1979. It was meant to be published as it stands. The book consisted of a general introduction to Caribbean music together with some history of the passage of black people from Africa via the West Indies to Great Britain. The main focus was on the origins and development of reggae music. In its original form and with its original title, *Rebel Sound: Reggae and Other Caribbean Music*, it was designed to stand on its own as one of a series of books on popular music aimed at young people at different ages and at various levels, doing courses in schools on general studies, communications, black studies, popular music or popular culture. I still hope the book will make sense in this context. The second version – what I've called the "Dub Version" – was written in 1982 for a book called *Reggae International* edited by Stephen Davis and Peter Simon (published in Britain by Thames & Hudson (1983)). "Ska Tissue: The Rise and Fall of Two Tone" was written as a short article on the British Two Tone movement aimed at a general readership. The third version – what I've called the "Club Mix" – was written in July, 1986, in an attempt to bring the whole thing up to date. I also wanted to use the opportunity to go back over some of the ground I'd covered in the "Original Cut" and "Dub" versions so that I could rework them from a different angle in the light of my current perspectives and interests. The "Club Mix" falls somewhere in between the first and second versions in terms of the imagined readership.

One of the characteristics of Afro-American and Caribbean music often cited by critics in a spirit of censure, is that there is too much stress on repetition and not enough "originality". There is a well documented tendency among classically trained, Eurocentric musicologists to write off black music as "repetitive" or "banal". This book, needless to say, is written against that critical tendency. It wouldn't be stretching the point to say that it is dedicated to the power and value of repetition. The very structure of the book *insists* on repetition. Far from seeing repetition as a wart to be removed from the face of the text, I see it as a beauty spot: repetition is the basis of all rhythm and rhythm is at the core of life.

I have tried to resist the temptation of changing the older texts: the original and dub mixes. They are embedded in their own time(s) and they should be read as historical documents rather than as authoritative statements. We always say both less and more than we mean to. (The triumphalist tone with which I haul in the Big Youth quote "No more songs about girls" at the end of Chapter Nine now just seems callow and silly ... I've changed as well as the music and the definition of "cultural politics" in the last seven years.) Having said that, I should add that I felt compelled in Chapter Nine to change the tenses because it is largely about Bob Marley, and Marley had died of cancer in the intervening period. When I went back to this project earlier this year, I'd intended to rewrite the chapter as an obituary. In the end I decided that wasn't appropriate or necessary. Bob Marley never did believe in death. He never had any time for it. He was too busy listening for the future and his interest in roots had nothing whatsoever to do with a morbid fascination for the past. Bob Marley would never have wanted the Forward March of his people or his people's music to falter for an instant just because he is no longer here in person. And the vital mix – Marley's voice and rhythms – are still with us. Apart from one or two minor modifications elsewhere, the "Original Cut" is as it stands in the original manuscript. The "Dub" remains intact.

This book, then, is an attempt to escape the Terror of the Book – that feeling of dread that stands alongside you as you sit down to write knowing full well that you're never going to know enough to get it right... It's an attempt to reproduce on paper the versioning process which has kept the combination of voice and rhythm in Caribbean music so crucial for so long. Not a just book, perhaps. Just a book...

Finally, I should add that I recognise that the title is misleading in another sense in that I don't deal adequately with all the music of the Caribbean (soca, for instance, hardly gets a mention) and I concentrate to what some might think an inordinate extent on Jamaican popular music. Even here I have left a great deal out. The book is by no means a comprehensive guide to reggae. All I can say is that I've written about the music to which I've felt personally drawn and which I've felt closest to. I offer no apology, by the way, for starting a book on Caribbean music with quotes from an American critic, Albert Goldman, on Elvis Presley, an American rock 'n' roll star. I'm sure that Lee "Scratch" Perry and Afrika Bambaata would understand the logic of the mix.

ORIGINAL CUT:
REBEL SOUND:
REGGAE & OTHER
CARIBBEAN MUSIC

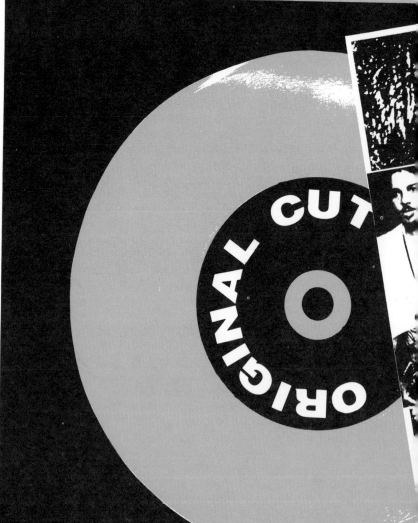

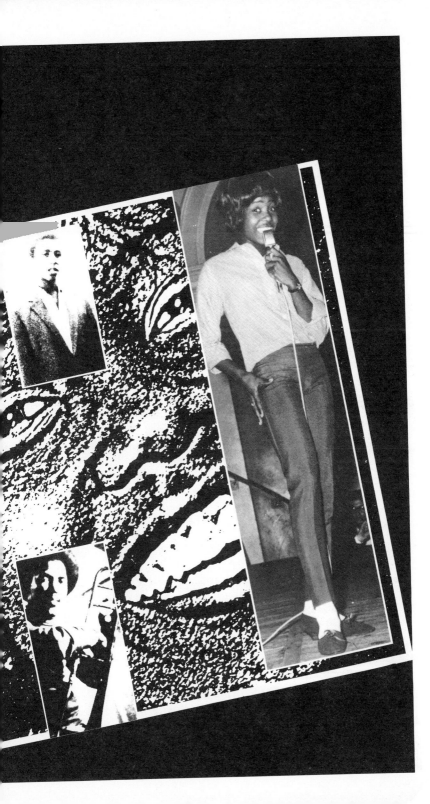

Original cut (1979)
(Rebel sound: reggae and other Caribbean music)

Introduction: the two Jamaicas

"If you are island hunting and you are looking for a subtropical climate, ivory white beaches, dramatic lush green mountains and superb hotels, then you need look no further than Jamaica... Jamaica is regarded by some to have the most breath-taking scenery in all the Caribbean. Take an excursion into the Blue Mountains... Gushing streams form a network down the mountain sides, creating spectacular waterfalls and finally reaching... the Caribbean sea... Jamaica has an exciting history beginning in 1494 to show you. Great plantation houses such as Brimmer Hall and Rose Hall have survived and are open to view. Charming mountain villages such as Mandeville, steepled churches, village greens and the counties of Middlesex, Cornwall and Surrey all strongly bring to mind the centuries of British rule.

... All the air-conditioned bedrooms in your hotel face the sea and have either a private patio or balcony. Your room will be attractively furnished with a shower and/or tub-bath... You can sail, or try your hand at snorkelling, scuba diving, water skiing or fishing, or stay on land and play tennis... In the evening there will be local entertainment, steel bands, calypso singers, limbo dancers and for the late nighters a discotheque..."

(P & O Cruises booklet, 1979)

"... Too many people living in oil drums and fruit crates and one-room plywood outhouses, with nothing except a formica dinette and a glass cabinet for the family china and a radio blasting. West Kingston literally is a garbage dump...

They built shacks and huts out of cardboard and plywood and rusty old iron, and the place spread... till now it's teeming. Kingston itself is in a basin, shut in by the Blue Mountains, and in the summer, when the sun fries the street and the asphalt begins to bubble and erupt and the dirt and zinc-dust and nameless vapours hang in the air, down in Trench Town and Jones Town and Tivoli Gardens... you choke.

... And still they come to town, gangling teenage runaways from the canefields and five-acre farms, all looking for something faster than chopping cane and humping bananas all their lives. Not sure... what they're really looking for at all – except they all know about Jimmy Cliff and Desmond Dekker and the rest of them. They were all just country boys running with the Rude Boys until they bluffed their way into Leslie Kong's record store with a little tune they'd written..."

(Jamaica: Babylon on a Thin Wire, *Michael Thomas*)

"Jamica, land of weed and water,
Motor vehicle and man-slaughter."
(No Chuck It by *Dillinger*, a reggae artist)

Jamaica... for most people living in Europe and the States the word probably conjures up a confused set of images – a patchwork of impressions derived from rum bottle labels, television and travel ads. This is the Jamaica of the travel brochures – a tropical paradise of white beaches, blue seas and swaying palms. And as far as history is concerned, there are the grand old plantation houses – stately reminders of the "centuries of British rule" (Jamaica was a British colony until 1962). An even more romantic picture of the island and its history can be found in childhood books and Hollywood adventure films. Here, the word "Jamaica" summons up a world of pirates and doubloons, of Captain Henry Morgan and the Brethren of the Coast holding the high seas to bloody ransom from Port Royal. And together these two versions blend to give us a picture of an enchanted island which, between its "colourful" past and carefree present, has experienced few real problems.

But there is another Jamaica – a different, more disturbing set of images. This is the *Other Side of Paradise* which Michael Thomas writes about in the extract above. Anyone who has listened to the lyrics of songs recorded by Jamaican reggae artists like Jimmy Cliff or Bob Marley will already be familiar with this other Jamaica. Marley has called it a "concrete jungle" – a twilight world of slums and shantytowns where the island's black population – the descendants of West African slaves – live out their lives in conditions which are a million miles away from the plush resorts of Ochos Rios and Montego Bay. Reggae has done much to publicise this image abroad. For reggae isn't just a set of highly danceable rhythms. The lyrics of reggae hits often stray far from the normal concerns of rock and pop music – problems with parents, boyfriends and girlfriends. With the new rhythm comes a powerful new message. The message is about poverty and inequality and black identity.

As Bob Marley, reggae's first truly international star, "chants down Babylon" and shakes his long, plaited dreadlocks on the stages and screens of Europe and America, he not only gives the world a new form of music. He puts that other Jamaica on display. In records like *Catch A Fire* and *Exodus*, he reveals what our travel brochures and history books hide – the roots of black Jamaican experience in slavery and colonialism.

It's hardly surprising that the brochures have tended to play down reggae music. For the tourists there are, instead, steel bands, jaunty calypsoes and brightly costumed limbo dancers. Reggae, "raw" reggae – the Trenchtown rock you can hear in downtown Kingston – would simply not fit in. And so the tourists and the "sufferers" are kept separate. They offer us different images – the official and unofficial versions of life in Jamaica. The two Jamaicas never meet. But the conflict between them is becoming more and more open.

In 1978 Peter Tosh, a founder member of the Wailers group, gave a performance at Jamaica's huge National Stadium. The place was filled to capacity and the crowd included both the island's Prime Minister and the leader of the opposition party. Striding on stage clad in a menacing black kung fu suit, beret and dark glasses, Tosh took the opportunity to make a passionate speech about the state of present-day Jamaica. He referred to men like John Hawkins and Sir Walter Raleigh – men whom the English history books have turned into heroes – as "slave-trading pirates". Before playing a set which included a song entitled *Get Up, Stand Up For Your Rights*, Tosh gave a final warning. There are still pirates in Jamaica, he said, only now they are called tourists, and instead of carrying cutlasses, they are armed with "little cameras round their necks".

If we are to understand how reggae and the tourist handbooks can present such different images of life in Jamaica, we have to go back into the history of the whole Caribbean. And if reggae or any of the other forms of West Indian music are really to make sense to us, we must first trace them back to their origins in Africa and Europe.

Chapter One

Slavery days

"Every time I hear the crack of the whip
My blood runs cold.
I remember on the slave ship
How they brutalise my very soul."
(Bob Marley and the Wailers, Catch A Fire*)*

"For sale: two mules, three goats, a sow with eight pigs and a
fine healthy woman with four children."
(Advertisement from a Barbadian newspaper, circa 1770)

The New World – the mainland of America together with the West
Indian Islands – was discovered by Christopher Columbus in 1492.
However, despite the fact that the area was settled by Europeans and
supplied Europe with many of its raw materials, at least three-
quarters of the present population of the West Indies are not of
European descent. Instead, they are the descendants of black slaves
who were forcibly taken from the West Coast of Africa and made to
work on the sugar plantations of the Caribbean islands during the
centuries of British rule.

The first people to be made slaves were the Carib and Arawak
Indians who lived on the islands before the Europeans arrived. And it
wasn't until the landowners began cultivating sugar in the 1600s that
large numbers of slaves from Africa were brought to the Caribbean.
Because the settlers grew their sugar on huge plantations, there was a
need for a large, disciplined workforce to tend and harvest the crop. It
was at that point that the slave trade was opened up. Although the
Portuguese were the first Europeans to exploit the West Coast of
Africa for slaves, the trade was soon dominated by the British.

Most of the Africans who worked on the West Indian sugar
plantations had originally been sold into slavery by other Africans.
They had either been captured during tribal wars, kidnapped by Arab
slavers, or taken during raiding parties organised for profit by local
chiefs. Once in European hands, the slaves were herded into the
cramped holds of the slave ships and chained together.[1]

The conditions on the ships were appalling. Some shipowners
reckoned on losing half their human cargo through sickness during
the long voyage. Things hardly improved once the ships had docked.

When they arrived in the West Indies, the slaves were lined up on the quayside like cattle and sold to the highest bidder. One slave, who managed to buy his freedom in 1776, wrote his own life-story, which included this account of a slave auction in Barbados:

> "On a signal given (as the beat of a drum) the buyers rush at once into the yard where the slaves are confined and make choice of that parcel they like best. The noise and clamour with which this is attended and the eagerness visible on the countenances of the buyers serves not a little to increase the apprehension of the terrified Africans. In this manner, without scruple, are relations and friends separated, most of them never to see each other again. I remember on the vessel in which I was brought over... there were several brothers who, in the sale, were sold in different lots, and it was very moving on this occasion to see and hear their cries at parting."

On their arrival at the plantations, those slaves who were not destined for work in the "Big House" (some plantation owners employed as many as forty house slaves) were set to work in gangs. They laboured on average from six till eleven in the morning and, after an hour's break, from twelve till dusk. They were housed in prison-like dwellings situated behind the ornate mansions of the masters and their families. Many slaves died soon after they arrived on the plantations during the period of acclimatisation – the "seasoning" in slaveowners' jargon. They succumbed to a variety of illnesses, which ranged from dysentery and smallpox to lockjaw and "despondency" – in plain language, the loss of the will to live.

Those who survived were closely supervised and any misconduct severely punished. Slaves who were considered surly or disobedient were flogged. Runaways were publicly whipped and often gibbeted and hung up to rot as a deterrent to any other slaves who hoped to seize their freedom in this way. Still, despite the harsh regime of field work and the continual supervision of whip-wielding overseers, many slaves did fight back. There is a long tradition in the West Indies of resistance to white rule – a tradition which stretches right back to the earliest days of slavery.

The *maroons* were the first black rebels on the islands. The word referred to runaway slaves who formed their own outlawed communities in the mountainous interiors of islands like St Kitts and Barbados. But the Jamaican maroons were the ones most feared by the British authorities. Under the leadership of a Coromantee warrior, Cujo, the Jamaican maroons held out against the British and colonial forces for almost fifty years. Eventually, in 1739, a treaty was signed ending the war. But in the traditional maroon townships of Cockpit County the exploits of Cujo and his people are still remembered with pride. When Stephen Davis visited the descendants of the original maroons in 1976 he was told that dances are still held to commemorate the old battles against the British. And during these dances, an old red coat, a British soldier's tunic "riddled with bullet holes and still boasting cutlass tears", is taken out and hoisted aloft in memory of former victories.[2]

The maroons were not the only Caribbean rebels. There were frequent slave outbreaks on most of the British islands from the seventeenth century onwards, though most of them were quickly put down and the leaders executed. However, there was a successful revolt on the French island of Saint Dominique in 1791. Under the leadership of the black general, Toussaint L'Ouverture, the slaves on this island rose up against their owners and drove them into the sea. And on 1 January, 1804, after a long campaign against the French, the rebel forces triumphed. Saint Dominique became Haiti, the first independent black republic in the Caribbean.

The last large slave revolt in the British West Indies occurred in Jamaica. In 1831, hundreds of slaves led by Sam Sharpe, a black Baptist minister, took up arms against the local militia. The uprising ended in the massacre by British troops of all those involved. But the rebellion helped to speed up the passing of a law banning slavery in the British colonies. In 1834, the Abolition Bill was passed in Westminster and 668,000 slaves were finally given their freedom.

However, life for most ex-slaves remained grim. They were understandably reluctant to work for their former masters, particularly as the plantation owners offered very low wages for field work. In an attempt to drive the ex-slaves back onto the plantations, the authorities imposed heavy taxes which hit especially hard at the black population . As a result, in 1865 there was another rebellion. Paul Bogle, (who was, like Sharpe, a black Baptist minister) led a rebel force against the mainly white township at Morant Bay. He was eventually captured and hanged, together with a wealthy coloured planter named George William Gordon. Gordon was accused of inciting the people to revolt by advocating self-government for Jamaican blacks. It was to take almost one hundred years for Gordon's dream to be fulfilled when finally, in 1962, Jamaica won her independence.

But the days of slavery have left an indelible mark on the island. Even in present-day Jamaica there are social and economic problems which can be traced back directly to the old plantation system. Jamaica's poverty, unemployment and racial and social inequality are all largely inherited from the past. It is the light-skinned "coloured" population who, for the most part, run the country. It is the Chinese, Syrians and Anglo-Indians who own many of the smaller shops and businesses. (They are descendants of the large numbers of Indians and Chinese who were "imported" after slavery was abolished to work on the sugar plantations.) And it is in the more manual jobs, or without a job at all, that you tend to find the black descendants of the West African slaves. Unemployment amongst this group runs very high indeed and many families live well below the bread line. Such poverty naturally breeds bitterness and anger, particularly amongst the young. For the black population it must seem that little has changed in Jamaica over the last 400 years. And if slavery appears to continue even now in only a slightly more subtle form, so too does that old Jamaican tradition of rebellion and resistance to authority...

Drums and concertinas

One of the less obvious ways in which the slaves fought back was through their music. Music was one of the means through which they could express their resentment, anger and frustration. From the time of the maroons the blowing of the *abeng* (cow horn) served as the signal for the slaves to take up arms. Other instruments helped the slaves in subtler ways. Drumming was particularly important. By preserving African drumming traditions, by remembering African rhythms, the slaves could keep alive the memory of the freedom they had lost. They could keep a part of themselves free from European influence.

At the same time they could adapt European forms of music and dance to suit their needs. The slaves didn't own the land on which they worked or the crops they grew. As far as the law was concerned, they didn't even own themselves. But they were free to take the masters' music. By adding African rhythms they could turn it into something which was exclusively their own.

In a fictional account of a slave voyage in his novel *Roots*, Alex Haley imagines how the slaves might first have heard white music and what it might have meant to them. We join the story at the point where Kunta Kinte, an African boy kidnapped by white slavers, is brought up for the first time from the ship's slave quarters to be exercised on deck. (The word *toubob* refers in the Mandinka language to the white men, the members of the ship's crew.)

> "The first open daylight in nearly fifteen days hit Kunta with the force of a hammer between the eyes. He reeled under the bursting pain, flinging his free hand up to cover his eyes...

... They were all being shoved and whipped towards where another chain of ten men was being doused with buckets of seawater drawn up from over the side. Then other toubob with long-handled brushes were scrubbing the screaming men. Kunta screamed too, as the drenching seawater hit him, stinging like fire in his bleeding whip cuts and the burned place on his back ... Then they were herded back towards the centre of the deck, where they flopped down in a huddle. Kunta gawked upwards to see toubob springing about on the poles like monkeys pulling at the many ropes among the great white cloths. Even in Kunta's shock, the heat of the sun felt warm and good, and he felt an incredible sense of relief that his skin was free of some of its filth.

... Then a toubob near the rail began pulling out and pushing in between his hands some peculiar folding thing that made a wheezing sound. Another joined in, beating on a drum from Africa, as other toubob now moved themselves into a ragged line, with the naked men, women and children staring at them. The toubob in the line had a length of rope and each of them looped one ankle within it, as if that rope was a length of chain such as linked the naked men. Smiling now, they began jumping up and down together in short hops, keeping in time with the drum beats and the wheezing thing. They and the other armed toubob gestured for the men in chains to jump in the same manner. But when the chained men continued to stand as if petrified, the toubobs' grins became scowls and they began laying about with whips.

... 'Jump!' shouted the oldest woman suddenly in Mandinka. She began jumping herself. 'Jump!' she cried shrilly again, glaring at the girls and children, and they jumped as she did. 'Jump to kill the toubob!' she shrieked, her quick eyes flashing at the naked men, her arms and hands darting in the movements of the warrior's dance. And then, as her meaning sank home, one after another shackled pair of men began a weak, struggling hopping up and down, their chains clanking against the deck. With his head man, Kunta saw the welter of hopping feet and legs, feeling his own legs rubbery under him as his breath came in gasps. Then the singing of the woman was joined by the girls. It was a happy sound, but the words they sang told how these terrible toubob had taken every woman into the dark corners of the canoe each night and used them like dogs. 'Toubob fa!' (kill toubob) they shrieked with smiles and laughter. The naked, jumping men joined in: 'Toubob fa!' Even the toubob were grinning now, some of them clapping their hands with pleasure."[3]

That episode is an imaginary one but it tells us a lot about Caribbean music. First, the music was the result of two different traditions – the African and the European – the meeting here of drums and concertinas. Most modern pop and rock, jazz, blues, soul and even reggae can be traced back to that blending of black and white forms. But the episode also sheds light on another aspect of the music produced by black people in the New World. On the surface it may sound light and carefree like the music on the ship. But underneath the harmonies and the bright, happy rhythms you can often hear those other voices – the angry threatening voices of the slaves and their descendants – the "rebel sound" of people seeking freedom or revenge.

Chapter Two

West African roots,
West Indian flowers

"My two grandfathers guard me
Lance with head of bone, drum of wood and leather:
My black grandfather.
Ruff wide at the throat, grey warrior's armour:
My white grandfather.
Naked feet, rocky torso
These from my black man.
Pupils of Antarctic glass,
These from my white man."
   (Nicholas Guillen, a Cuban mulatto [Afro-European] poet)

The slaves who were brought to the West Indies came from a number of different tribes. Some came from very developed societies with complex systems of government and large-scale farming. Others were used to more primitive conditions – scratching a living from the barren soil by grazing cattle. Each tribe had its own particular identity, its own forms of religion and art. Some tribes specialised in pottery, others in weaving or leather goods. Still others had developed skills in bronze and copper work.

Each tribe brought its own traditions and beliefs and spoke its own language. But in general, the slave-owners did not like to see communication between the slaves. Talk could lead to revolt. So the slaves were discouraged from speaking, reading and writing. At times, on the English islands, they were even banned from attending Christian church services just in case they used the opportunity to band together against their masters.

Nevertheless, the slaves managed to preserve their tribal traditions. Throughout the eighteenth and nineteenth centuries, slaves on most of the Caribbean islands formed clubs which were called "nations". These were organised along tribal lines and each nation was pledged to preserve its own African language and religion. Although the authorities tried to stamp them out, the network of nations continued, in some cases, well into the twentieth century. On Grenada you can still see the Nations Dance. And in 1978, a visitor to the Mardi Gras Carnival in New Orleans (USA) recorded a Nations chant in which bands of local blacks grouped in "tribes" and dressed as Red Indians were led in song by a Big Chief.[1] In this particular case, the original dance had been banned since 1817. But the slaves had managed to keep the tradition alive by adopting Red Indian fancy dress to avoid prosecution. Like Kunta Kinte and the other dancing Africans on the slave ship, they had had to resort to secrecy and disguise in order to keep their beliefs and customs.

One of the things which united the slaves was religion and religious music. The different tribal religions shared common themes. For many tribes certain features of the natural world – such as animals and trees – were held sacred. And most West Africans also worshipped their ancestors. Similarly, though each tribe brought its own musical traditions, there were features common to all West African music.

First, the slaves' music was likely to be dominated by the drums: they are still the central instruments in West Africa. Those and the percussion instruments – the clappers, scrapers, bells and rattles which cut across the rhythmic foundation supplied by the big basses and the tom-toms are what make the music of the area so distinctive.

The second feature common to all traditional West African music is that it serves an important social function. As one writer puts it, music acts as a "social glue", binding the people together as a group. Every member of the tribe, even those who are not especially skilled musically, can participate – perhaps by shaking a gourd containing a small pebble to keep time, or by following the rhythm with their feet in dances which have changed little over the centuries.

There is music for every occasion. There are work songs, songs for births, marriages and deaths, songs to celebrate victories over enemies or to inspire warriors going into battle. And there are special songs in which prominent members of the tribe are praised or criticised and insulted. All these songs depend heavily on the drums. And particularly in religious music, the rhythms can become extremely complex – so complex, in fact, that one European listener has compared the sound to "water dropping over a cliff onto a stone ledge".[2] Each percussion instrument makes its own unique contribution to the overall sound. In these ways, each event in the life of the tribe has a rhythm which can be immediately identified.

For the slaves in the West Indies, religion and music became even more closely related than they had been in Africa. Slaves from different tribes could find common ground in shared religious beliefs. The sound of drumming and the chanting of the religious cults began to summon up the planters' worst fears – that one day the blacks might recognise their strength as a group and rise up against their masters, as they had done in Haiti. As a result, the forbidden religious rituals were driven underground.

But they refused to die away completely. On many islands, the West African *cumina* cult flourished amongst the slaves for centuries, even though it was generally banned. One Christian missionary observed the following *cumina* rite in Jamaica in the late 1700s:

> "As soon as darkness of evening set in [the slaves] assembled in crowds in open pastures, most frequently under large cotton trees, which they worshipped and counted holy. After sacrificing some fowls, the leader began an extempore song, in a wild strain, which was answered in chorus – the dance grew wilder until they were in a state of excitement bordering on madness. Some would perform incredible revolutions while in this state, until, nearly exhausted, they fell senseless to the ground when every word they uttered was received as divine revelation."

But these pure African survivals are rare. In most cases the slaves had to adopt and modify their music and beliefs to comply with the colonial laws and slave codes. On the French and Spanish islands where the official religion was Roman Catholicism, the slaves were actually forced to become Christians, although once again they adapted the Catholic religion to fit in with their own beliefs. So there grew up a whole range of cults which mixed together aspects of Christian and West African worship.

In Brazil there were the cults of *santeria*, *umbanda* and *candomble*. In Cuba and Trinidad, the slaves went on worshipping the West African god, *Shango*. And in Haiti there was *voodoo*. In all these cults, Catholic saints were made to *stand in* for the various African gods. The switch was usually simple: for black slaves in Brazil, Ogun, the African god of iron, became St Anthony, while for the slaves in Cuba he was linked to John the Baptist. Larry Harlow, a Cuban musician, explains how the system worked:

> "The slaves . . . weren't allowed to worship their gods openly so they prayed to a Catholic saint and they'd take St Barbara – an image of a woman – and yet they'd be singing to this big black man – whom they called Shango who was the god of virility and thunder."[3]

There were other similarities between the various cults. Each had candle-lit ceremonies in which members of the congregation were suddenly possessed or "ridden" by the spirits of their African ancestors.

Despite the efforts of the Christian churches, the mixed cults of the Caribbean still survive today. In Haiti, it's been estimated that ninety-five per cent of the present population still believe in voodoo. And, strangest of all, in Cuba where religion officially no longer exists because Cuba has been a communist state since 1959, the forbidden cults of *Shango* and *santeria* continue to flourish. At least that's what an islander told one recent European visitor:

> "Everyone believes here in Cuba. Look, see that guy with sort of sacking pants. He's wearing them for Baba-al-aye, that's Saint Lazarus. And that woman we saw, she had a red and white necklace. She's a daughter of Shango [that is, she is a devotee of the cult]. Those are his colours, red and white. Blood and bandages. You'll see necklaces like that on even very high up people in the government. Or a little thing of beads round the ankle. Cubans can't live without it, *santeria*, black and white . . ."[4]

So it's possible even now to find a midnight ceremony in progress in some remote part of Cuba or Haiti. And in the background, above the strange, eerie moans of the possessed, you can hear the complicated rhythms of West African religious drumming, still essentially unchanged.

But the influence of these rhythms on West Indian life stretches far beyond these cults, since they provide the basis for much non-religious music in the Caribbean. All the dances associated with Cuba – the most famous is the rumba – can be traced back to the black religions and black religious rhythms. They all had their origins in *Shango* or *santeria*. In the same way, you can still hear *voodoo* songs in Haiti which go right back to Africa. And many *voodoo* drummers play in a traditional West African way – squatting over their drums and changing the pitch by rubbing their bare heels across the goatskin surface.

It's not surprising that the African connection should be clearest in Haiti. For almost 200 years, Haiti has been relatively free of direct European influences. So the Haitian authorities have generally shown more tolerance towards African music and religions than elsewhere in the Caribbean. But this wasn't always so.

For many years after the revolution of 1804, Haiti was ruled by a lightskinned (Afro-European) elite. These coloured rulers tended to share the preferences of the old French colonists whom they replaced. For this reason Catholicism with its European connections remained for many years the official religion in Haiti. And *voodoo* (which was associated with Africa) was banned from time to time. As a reaction against this, a number of black Haitian writers and artists got together in the 1930s and formed a group called the *Griots*. (In West Africa, the griot is the story teller who hands down the tribal customs from generation to generation.)

The Griots set out to make black Haitians proud of their African roots. They wanted Haitians to value being black instead of being ashamed of the fact. So they began glorifying all things African. No member of the griot group had in fact actually set foot in Africa, so they had to rely on ideas and *images* of Africa handed down to them by the white man. And of course many of these images were crude and inaccurate. They gave the impression that Africa was a savage place – inferior to Europe in every way – a "Dark Continent".

And so a myth of Africa grew up – a white man's myth. Now the Haitian Griots took up this myth too, but they did so in a completely different spirit. They valued everything that the Europeans had despised. Instead of looking down on Africa as a "backward" place, they welcomed the fact that it was untainted by what the Europeans called "civilisation". As an extreme example of this, one of the group, Carl Brouard, wrote a poem entitled *Nostalgie*. In this poem he says that when he hears the sound of the drum, his soul goes back to Africa where he sits in a hut and drinks blood out of human skulls. Other members of the group also used deliberately shocking images like this when describing Africa and their relationship to it. It was as if they were using the myth that Africa was a barbaric place to wipe out the memory of "civilised" Europe. After all, the main thing that Europe's civilisation had given *them* was slavery.

The myth of Africa continues even now in the West Indies. It tends to crop up as a positive force when a group of people like the Griots are trying to establish a new identity for their countries – one which is free of all European influences. And we shall meet the myth again in certain types of reggae music.

However, Haiti is not typical of the Caribbean as a whole. Its music and religion are too purely African. On most islands, a new West Indian culture was born out of the meeting of Europe and Africa. Even new West Indian languages were produced in this way. Most black West Indians speak a version of English called "patois". This is a combination of seventeenth-century servants' English and various African languages. As a result, patois sounds quite different from standard BBC English. Most of the quotations from reggae artists in this book come from interviews in Jamaican patois. The same kind of thing happened on the French-speaking islands. Only there, the slaves spoke a dialect which mixed together French and various African tongues.

In a similar way, most Caribbean music has come to contain European as well as African elements. For instance, the Latin sound of Cuba which has been popular throughout the world since the 1930s consists basically of Spanish melodies and African rhythms – "the love affair of African drums and Spanish guitars", as one writer puts it. Nonetheless, even in Cuban music, the rhythms – the African contribution – tend to dominate. This is what makes the Caribbean sound so different from most other forms of pop. Machito, a Cuban band leader who played with American musicians for many years, noted the difference when comparing Cuban music and American jazz:

> "In Cuban music, we never complicate the melody. It is the rhythm that is rich. But in jazz you have all the interest on top of the rhythm – everything is happening at the top. Our music is different. It all occurs at the bottom in the rhythm. Let me give you a better definition. When there's a storm, then the thunder and lightning represent jazz, the American music. But when there's an earthquake, that's Cuban music. The rhythm moves you because it is where you are standing. You have to dance."[5]

Ultimately, all West Indian music places the emphasis on the rhythm rather than the melody. Even where the European influence is strong, as in the music of Cuba or Trinidad, you can still hear that beat – the distinctive flow and shuffle which makes the music so good to dance to. As we'll see, reggae is largely a matter of rhythm – each new phase in the music has been produced by a slight rhythmic change. And as we shall see in the next chapter on Trinidad, rhythm, being so important to the music and to the sense of identity of the black population, was such a sensitive topic that at times it became a political issue.

Chapter Three

The music of Trinidad

Trinidad has a very chequered history. Like many of the Caribbean islands, it was originally settled by the Spanish in the 1500s. But at the end of the eighteenth century, the Spanish government invited Catholics from the French West Indies to settle there. Finally, in 1797, Trinidad and the smaller sister island of Tobago became British colonies. Trinidad remained so until 1962. Apart from these European influences, the slaves added their own African strand. And, as in Jamaica, there is also a large Chinese and East Indian population – the descendants of field labourers brought to the island by the British in the 1800s. There is even a small community of the original Caribbean Indians in the south.[1]

Every year in Trinidad, for the two days leading up to Ash Wednesday, all the island's people come together to celebrate Carnival. Work stops, and from five o'clock on Monday morning till midnight on Tuesday, the streets of Port of Spain, the capital city, throb to the rhythms of the steel bands and calypsoes. Carnival – or "mas" (masquerade) as it's called in Trinidad – is taken very seriously indeed. There are brightly coloured costumes, competitions, prizes and, of course, non-stop dancing. For without steel band and calypso there would be no Carnival. In fact, the history of Trinidad's music and its mas are all bound up together. And, as so often in the West Indies, both the music and the celebrations came originally out of the poor black areas – out of the experience of the slaves and their descendants.

Carnival had its origins in the European tradition of the masquerade. Every year Trinidad's wealthy French people would parade through the streets wearing masks and greeting passers-by. After 1838, the emancipated slaves celebrated their freedom by taking over this tradition. On the Sunday before Carnival, horns were blown to summon the island's black population, and they would march in procession through the streets of Port of Spain to the beat of the goatskin drum.

These processions were called *canboulays* because the marchers carried lighted torches (the word comes from the French *cannes brulées*, meaning burning canes). On the surface, these processions seemed harmless enough. They appeared to derive from the old custom of assembling the slaves at night to put out fires on the plantations. But they also held a more sinister meaning as far as the island's whites were concerned. In the more remote parts of the island, the burning of the cane signalled to the slaves that a forbidden *Shango* ceremony was in progress. Needless to say, when the *canboulay* came to Port of Spain, the European residents began to feel a little uneasy.

Once again, the white observers found the African survivals most unsettling. The memory of the Haitian revolt and its voodoo connections were still fresh in the minds of local Europeans. To their eyes, Carnival looked dangerously like a riot. For instance, one report in 1870 described the festivities as little more than "unremitting uproar, yelling, drumming and the blowing of horns". Inevitably there was a move to suppress the event. Drumming and the Shango religion were banned. Then in 1881 the fears of the authorities were confirmed in the canboulay riots. A new police chief, Captain Baker, had just been appointed and he was determined to stamp out any signs of public disorder during Carnival. He was particularly opposed to the custom of stick-fighting which was a central part of the festivities. Stick-fighting, as the name suggests, was a contest of strength and skill. It was probably African in origin, but it had been revived by the slaves in Trinidad. During mas, bands of twenty or more field hands led by "big pappies" and armed with long fighting sticks, would roam the city streets. When they came across rival groups they would throw down challenges in warlike songs called *calindas* and fights would follow. When Captain Baker assumed office, he set out to crush the sport.

As the police converged on the procession, there was a full-scale battle. After driving the police back, the crowd lit fires and buried an effigy of Captain Baker in a mock funeral. Gradually, order was restored but as a result of the riot, stick-fighting was finally banned. It was forbidden for more than ten men together to carry sticks.

However, as usual, people found ways of getting round the colonial laws. For most of the year, they confined their stick-fighting sessions to the yards of the slums. But during Carnival, they managed to preserve the tradition in a disguised form by setting up *tambour-bamboo* bands. These bands were made up of musicians carrying lengths of bamboo cut to various sizes (up to three feet long for the bass notes). The bamboo sticks were either banged together or thumped on the ground to provide percussion for the Carnival songs. Of course, in the right hands, an instrument like this could become a highly effective weapon. Eventually, the *tambour-bamboo* bands were also stamped out.

From the 1890s onwards, the authorities tried to clean up Carnival. *The canboulay* processions were phased out, and fancy

dress and musical competitions were introduced by local businessmen with a view to "improving the moral tone of Carnival". But
the old tradition of resistance to authority still lingers on beneath the
surface. It has simply taken new and more subtle forms. And
although it may seem strange that the music which has made Carnival
famous throughout the world can be traced back to the warlike
customs of the stick-fighting bands, such is the case with both calypso
and steel bands.

The steel bands

The connection between stick-fighting and the steel bands is quite
direct. After the *tambour-bamboo* bands were stamped out, Carnival
was left without a rhythm section. People would keep time by tapping
kettles or bottles with metal spoons. But in 1937, there was a new
departure. A band from New Town caused a sensation with their
float based on the theme of the jazz hit *Alexander's Rag Time Band*.
The band's success that year was due only partly to the popular
theme. It was the band's use of rhythm which really made the
difference. By raiding kitchens and rubbish dumps, they had
collected together a formidable range of buckets, frying pans, oil
drums and dustbin lids to make up the first "orchestra of steel". They
not only won most of the prizes, they had also invented a sound which
since then has always been associated with Carnival – the clear,
mellow sound of the steel band.

For the next three years, steel bands were featured in the Carnival
processions. And then, in 1941, the US Navy were granted two bases
on the island. Carnival was officially suspended for the duration of
the Second World War. Or rather, it was driven underground.
Throughout the war, Carnival was secretly celebrated in the slum
yards of Port of Spain. And it was here that the "panmen" began to
develop and refine their techniques. They experimented by dividing
up the dustbin lid into sections to produce different notes. Eventually
they settled on the famous pattern which still forms the basis of the
modern steel band.

After the war, steel bands containing a number of accomplished
musicians emerged. But the music was still regarded as disreputable
and low class. The panmen began to gain a reputation as tough and
dangerous delinquents. Soon steel bands and trouble became firmly
linked in the public mind. And the magistrates seemed determined to
hand out a maximum fine or prison sentence to any panman found
guilty of even the most trivial offence.

It's tempting to trace the tough-guy image of the early panmen
back via the *tambour-bamboo* bands to the original stick-fighters.

During the 1940s and 1950s, rival panmen and their supporters fought pitched battles rather like their stick-fighting predecessors. These conflicts came to a head in the 1956 Carnival when two bands – Tokyo and the Invaders – took the "war" to the streets in a battle which lasted for hours.

But at the same time the panmen were developing their steel band instruments, and producing more and more subtle and delicate combinations of sound. Eventually, the dustbin lids were replaced by oil drums and the preparation of the pans began to take time and considerable skill. Now there is a standard procedure. First the drums are cut to various sizes and the unopened end is sunk to the required level with a sledgehammer. Next the pan is fired and tempered with oil, and finally tuned with a hammer and chisel. The steel bands also grew in size (some contain as many as 200 musicians) and are now divided into three main sections. The "ping pong" (or soprano) pans supply the melody. Harmony is added by the larger pans which are called the "guitar", "cello" and "bass" pans. Finally, the groundbeat is provided by cymbals, scratchers and drums, which can now be played quite openly at Carnival.

Steel band music is now thoroughly respectable. Even classical compositions are played by the massive orchestras of steel (the panmen call the classics "bomb tunes"). Panmen are no longer thought of as criminals. And juvenile delinquents are actively encouraged by the government to join the bands as a way of keeping them *out* of trouble. But the names of the famous panmen and the places they come from – Neville Jules and Fish Eye Olivierre from Hellyard, Winston "Spree" Simon from John John, Patch Eye Pajotte from Hill Sixty – tell a different story. They still manage to conjure up a slightly less worthy image. And if you listen closely you can still hear the clatter of the sticks behind the melodious ring of modern steel band music.

Calypso

> "They want to licence my mouth
> They don't want me to talk.
> But if is blood, sweat and misery
> We mean to fight till we get our liberty."

Calypso was the first Trinidadian music to break through to an audience beyond the West Indies. However, its exact origins are not known. Like Cuban music, it seems to combine African rhythms and European melodies. The main European contribution is probably Spanish, though it's been suggested that the first calypsonian was a

French speaking slave called Gros Jean. The African roots are no clearer. There are elements of slave digging songs. African work songs, Shango songs and songs sung by the slaves during revolts. And, like most forms of black music in the New World, calypso is based on the African "call and response" pattern. American blues, soul and jazz, Jamaican reggae and Trinidad's calypsoes all share this same basic structure. In African call and response, one person will sing a line and the rest will respond by singing a fixed chorus. Again, the call and response pattern shows how music in West Africa involves the whole community – everyone can join in. And calypsoes have the same structure too – each verse ends with a repeated chorus which the crowd soon learns to recognise.

But calypso has other more specifically Trinidadian sources as well. It grew like the steel bands out of the old stick-fighting sessions. As we've already seen, the "big pappies" and their supporters would sing defiant *calindas* before fighting. These were full of extravagant boasts and insults. Rather like the boasts of the black American boxer, Muhammed Ali, they served to unsettle the opponent. The boast *calinda*, too, is of African origin. But in Trinidad, where the slaves spoke a French-based patois, they were called the *sans humanités*, which in French means "without humanity".

The calypso continued the *sans humanité* tradition. Songs in this style were particularly popular during the 1930s and 1940s. Singers like Roaring Lion and Lord Executor would mock and challenge their rivals in song. For example, the following verses are taken from a calypso by Executor. In this song, he ridicules another lesser talent called Houdini:

> "The earth a-trembling and a-tumbling and heavens are
>   falling
> And all because the Lion is roaring.
> My tongue is like the blast of a gun,
> When I frown monarchs are going to bow down to the
>   ground.
> Devastation, destruction, desolation and damnation
> All these I'll inflict on insubordination.
>
> With my glittering sword in hand
> Tell Houdini
> This is the hour of destiny in this colony."

As in this example, Biblical language was often used. In Executor's song there are references to the Lion of Judah and the Day of Judgement. But the effect is always comic rather than threatening. Still, even though the boasts are not intended seriously, they do recall the old stick-fighting days. Even now, the leading calypso stars adopt a strutting, outlaw pose like the "big pappies". For instance, Mighty Sparrow, Trinidad's most popular calypsonian, draws on the stickman style. And calypso singers often give themselves jokey names and titles (like Mighty Spoiler) which strongly bring to mind the old traditions of the boast song.

Calypso also inherited the stick-fighting tradition of defiance to authority. From the earliest days, the calypso singers used to lace their lyrics with obscenities, blasphemies and attacks on the colonial authorities. To begin with, these gestures of defiance went unnoticed. As we have seen, they were lost on white ears and were dismissed as African "yelling" or Creole "noise". It was only in the 1890s when calypsoes began to be sung in English that the authorities started objecting to the lyrics. From then on, there were many attempts at official censorship. Calypso lyrics were published in the press, for Europeans to read before Carnival. And at one point it was even suggested that calypsoes should be submitted to the police for prior approval.

Gradually, as Carnival became more organised and orderly, so too did the calypso competitions which take place in the weeks leading up to the festivities. In the early days, the competitions were held in dirty, ill-equipped marquees. But in the 1920s, Chieftain Douglas, a railway ticket collector, put up a spacious, comfortable tent where he performed calypsoes nightly with his band The Railway Millionaires. Slowly, the old *picong* (improvised) calypsoes, which were rough and often loud, gave way to more complicated songs with more involved, witty lyrics.

In the 1930s, New York record companies discovered calypso and recorded the more popular numbers. These records were aimed at a wider, international market. And the lyrics were tailored to appeal to non-West Indian audiences. Eventually, in the 1940s, a white singing trio had a massive hit with a cover version of Lord Invader's *Rum and Coca Cola* – a calypso which originally satirised American sailors stationed in Trinidad. All the satire was taken out in the American version. And to add insult to injury, Lord Invader received no payment though the record sold more than five million copies.

These diluted calypsoes bore little relation to the raw island product. Trinidadians from the Port of Spain slums continued to poke fun at those in power and the tradition of open defiance reached its peak in the early 1940s in the songs of Attila the Hun. Attila's calypsoes tended to consist of long attacks on the Crown Colony regime. Their popularity gives some indication of just how deeply British rule was resented in Trinidad at the time.

During the War, when the American sailors were on the island, a new strain of protest worked itself out in calypso. A string of hits like

Spoiler's *Marabella Pork Vendor* and Growler's *Ding Dong Dell* dominated the Carnivals of the late 1940s and 1950s. These songs glorified the exploits of the "saga boys" and "glamour boys" – young pimps and delinquents who ran the red light district in Port of Spain. Many of the songs were hostile to the well-paid Americans who were taking away the saga boys' women.

One singer who grew out of this shady environment was Mighty Sparrow (real name Francisco Slinger). He won his first calypso crown in 1956 with a saga boy song called *Jean and Dinah*. This song celebrated the departure of the Americans with the boast: "It's the glamour boys again/We're going to rule Port of Spain". In his early career, Sparrow produced a number of calypsoes with strong social protest themes. In particular, he attacked the Americans who had opened up an oil refinery on the island at Point à Pierre. Sparrow accused the Americans of exploiting West Indian people. As far as he was concerned, they were just as bad as the old European colonists:

> "Well the days of slavery back again,
> I hope it ain't reach in Port of Spain.
> Since the Yankees come back over here
> They buy out the whole of Point à Pierre.
> Money start to pass, people start to bawl
> Point à Pierre sell the workmen and all."

Immediately after Independence in 1962, there was a weakening of the old tradition of social criticism. But since 1968 it has been revived once more by a former school teacher who calls himself the Mighty Chalkdust. Chalkdust attacked government inefficiency and corruption in songs like *Brain Drain* and *Goat Mouth*. In his calypso *Ah Fraid Karl*, for example, Chalkdust satirised the Attorney General, Karl Phillips, who had just passed a Sedition Act. One of Phillips' aims was to silence criticism of the government. However, Chalkdust manages to get round the law:

> "They say a young minster was found
> In a hotel with a call-girl in town
> But I ain't singing 'bout that
> Ah fraid the Sedition Act."

Chalkdust and other younger singers, such as the Mighty Stalin and the Lord Valentino, have managed to dethrone the Mighty Sparrow once or twice at recent Carnivals.

Sparrow's popularity still runs high and his contribution to calypso cannot be ignored. While he has largely abandoned social protest lyrics for love songs and sexual "boasts", he still produces the occasional searing satire on the present Trinidadian regime.

However, his real importance lies in his international popularity. Sparrow has helped to make calypso acceptable to a wider, whiter audience. Perhaps the lyrics have suffered as a result. Yet present-day calypso may not be quite as harmless as it sounds. It has learnt to hide its menace under bouncy, sunny rhythms. But behind the smiles of the singers in the satire and the bitter jokes of Trinidad's traditional calypsoes, there is a backlog of resentment to the colonial regime. As the tourists sit and smile at Sparrow's humorous delivery and bob up and down to the beat of his calypsoes, one is perhaps reminded of Kunta Kinte's toubob, clapping and jumping alongside the Africans on the slave ship – oblivious to the sinister meaning of the songs their slaves are singing.

Chapter Four

Reggae and other Caribbean music

Reggae has much in common with other forms of Caribbean music. It is, like calypso and Cuban music, a product of the union of African rhythms and European melody and harmony. As with Haitian music, there are some pure African survivals in reggae. You can find elements of African work songs and digging tunes – chants based on the call and response pattern of African communal singing. Other African survivals in Jamaica have also played their part in shaping reggae's unique sound. In the Blue Mountains, you can still hear African *anansi* songs, which tell the comic exploits of the spider, Brer Anansi. Similarly, the John Canoe *(Junkanoo)* dancers still perform in rural Jamaica at Christmas time. Dressed in rags and feathers they have preserved African rhythms and flute music. The strange name seems to stem from the African words *dzong kunu*, which mean "terrible sorcerer".

But Jamaican and Haitian music can be compared in other ways too. Many reggae records, especially those with a strong Rastafarian influence, are deeply concerned with the issues of black pride and black identity. And, as we've seen, these were the themes which preoccupied the Griot group in Haiti during the 1940s.

But it is Trinidad's music which is closest to reggae. In reggae there is the same emphasis on social criticism and political protest. There are the same "insult" and "boasting" traditions. And there is the same "roots" connection with the city slums. John John and Hellyard in Port of Spain, where calypso and the steel bands started, sound little different from Kingston's Trench Town and Back o' Wall which gave birth to reggae. The Israel Vibrations, a Jamaican reggae trio, began as a group of social outcasts tapping out their rhythms on tin cans, just like the early steel band musicians of Trinidad.

Now reggae, like Trinidad's music, has become a little more respectable. And, in both cases in recent years, politicians have tried to use the music for their own ends. Dr Eric Williams, Trinidad's Prime Minister, used the street-style of calypso for his famous speech "Massa Day Done" – the Days of the White Plantation Owner are Over. And, in exactly the same way, Michael Manley, Jamaica's Prime Minister, took his election slogans – "Better Must Come" and "Under Heavy Manners" – from reggae records and used reggae in his campaigns. But the musicians allowed neither Manley nor Williams to get away scot-free with such blatant propaganda. In a reggae song called *When Will Better Come?*, Junior Byles challenged the Jamaican Prime Minister to fulfil his election promises. Meanwhile, in Trinidad, the Mighty Chalkdust goaded Eric Williams with his own slogan in the calypso *Massa Day* Must *Done*, in which the singer points out there is still racial prejudice on the island.

In fact, there are direct links between calypso and Jamaican music. Before ska, the only folk music on the island was *mento*. This was a local version of calypso, though Jamaican *mento* lyrics were not generally as witty and controversial as those of Trinidad's calypsoes. But there are broader and deeper similarities between reggae and other Caribbean music. Most importantly, we find in Jamaica the same links between drumming, religion and resistance to the authorities. In the next chapter we shall be looking at these underground traditions to try to uncover the roots of reggae music. But first we'd better find out exactly what reggae is.

Reggae is . . .

"Reggae is Jamaican soul music, a sort of tropic rock 'n' roll with the accents on the second and fourth beats."

(*Stephen Davis*, writer)

"Reggae is protest formed out of suffering . . . You vibrate it back to those who oppress you. What I was playing was what I felt, y'know? . . . Hardship played out of the horn."

(*Rico Rodriguez*, Jamaican trombonist)

"Reggae is just coming from the people, y'know? Like a everyday t'ing. Like the ghetto. So all of our music, our Jamaican rhythm, comin' from the majority. Everyday t'ing that people use like food. We just put music to it and mek a dance out of it, y'know . . . When you say 'reggae' you mean *regular*, majority . . . It's the music from the rebels, people who don't have what they want."

(*Toots Hibbert*, reggae singer, and leader of the Maytals)

"It is the black Rastaman line of message to the world."
(*Ras. Michael* reggae singer, drummer and leader of the Sons of Negus)

"Reggae is an offshot of Rasta music. You see 'reggae' is a derivative of the Latin 'Regis' meaning 'King'. It is the music of the King for the King by the King."   (A Rastafarian)

"Popular Jamaican music was essentially a response to rhythm and blues which was the music that the radio stations were playing."

(*Dermot Hussey*, a Jamaican record producer)

"I think it's the same as jazz, with the same feeling as jazz."

(*Big Youth*, reggae "talk over" artist)

"We've always believed that reggae is no different from any other field except that it does need slightly different promotion and marketing techniques."

(A Virgin record company executive)

"Reggae is a religion to me."

(*David Hinds*, member of the UK reggae band Steel Pulse)

As you can see, it's difficult to say exactly what reggae is. But we do know some facts for certain. To begin with, the word "reggae" referred to a particular phase in Jamaican pop music. There were other phases, other slightly different rhythms before reggae, namely ska and rocksteady. And in recent years there have been a number of shifts – a number of new rhythms. All of these have been given names (e.g., "clappers", "rockers", "steppers") by those closest to the Jamaican sound. But "reggae" is the word that's stuck as far as the wider public is concerned. It has come to stand for virtually all forms of popular music in Jamaica.

In fact, the name first appeared in 1968 on a song recorded by Toots and the Maytals entitled *Do the Reggay*. Here it referred to a new dance – and a new sound. Reggae was distinguished from earlier Jamaican music by the way in which the rhythm and bass guitars were featured. The first thing you hear when listening to reggae is the jagged, "chikka-chikka" guitar rhythm (sometimes called the chicken-scratch) which seems to cut against the hypnotic, grumbling bass. Although Jamaican music goes on developing, it remains, at least at the moment, tied to this basic format. To introduce yet one more definition, the Jamaica Tourist Board issued a pamphlet containing the following "recipe" for reggae:

"One part rocksteady, one part mento, a hint of ska tempo, mix well in the heat of West Kingston, bring to the boil with an increasing social consciousness, and you have reggae."

We'll be looking in detail at ska and rocksteady later, but for the moment let's just take the last ingredient – the "increasing social consciousness". Part of that consciousness has grown up around the search for reggae's roots. Many reggae musicians deliberately draw on African traditions in their music. Reggae is at present filled with the themes and "ridims" (patois for "rhythms") of the Rastafarian movement. The Rastas stress pride in the African heritage. Indeed, in recent years, "roots reggae" with its references to "dread" and "ganja" (marijuana) has even become something of a cliché.

Cat Coore of the Jamaican group, Third World, is aware of this and is trying to move reggae away from its preoccupation with the "roots". He wishes to blend reggae with other musical forms, such as black American soul:

> "As soon as you mention reggae music most people think that you must come in dirty jeans, militant khaki shirt, a hat like Bob Marley and all that. No man. That's plain foolishness. Reggae music must be able to reach a man from every part of society. That is what Third World is all about."[1]

Coore may be right. Reggae may have lost a little of its early edge and drive in recent years because the whole question of the roots has been allowed to dominate. But on the other hand, reggae's power and appeal has always depended on its refusal to compromise for a large white audience. And part of its strength has stemmed from its concern with the past. So the "roots" remain important. They are, in the words of Stephen Davis, the "bloodlines" beating back to Africa and on towards the record-buying public of Europe and the States.

Chapter Five

The roots of reggae: religion
and religious music

",,, to keep the people together there was the Bible."
(*I Roy*, a reggae artist)

"The Bible is the history of your future." (*Bob Marley*)

We have already seen how slave revolts and uprisings were often linked to religious movements. In Jamaica, many of the rebellions were led by Christian preachers (e.g., Sam Sharpe, Paul Bogle, George William Gordon). Many slaves, after they were freed, joined the non-conformist Church congregations – such as the Baptists and Methodists – because they recognised that these churches had played an important part in the fight for Abolition. The non-conformist Churches also appealed to the former slaves because the services had much in common with traditional African forms of worship. The Baptist Church, in particular, is informal. As well as singing hymns, members of the congregation often dance and shout and sometimes "speak in tongues". And there is a good deal of rapport – of two-way conversation – between the preacher and his flock.

So it was easy for the slaves to insert the old African call and response pattern into the Christian service. Instead of just sitting quietly and listening to the minister, the congregation would add to or cut across his sermon with their own responses. In this way, the preacher could "ride" the developing mood. He could give voice to the feelings and fears and hopes of the people. And together, preacher and congregation formed a bond.

This type of service is really an extension of the pattern that we saw earlier in Trinidad's calypsoes. And it can be found in many other areas of public life in black communities throughout the Caribbean and the States. For example, in a magazine article entitled "Martin Luther King is still on the case", Garry Wills describes a speech delivered by the Reverend James Bevel to a black audience from Memphis. The meeting had been called immediately after the assassination in 1968 of Dr Martin Luther King, the black American civil rights leader, and feelings in the black community were running very high indeed. You can see how the call and response pattern works in the way the Reverend and his congregation relate to one another. In the following extract, Garry Wills' own observations have been put in brackets. At the point where we join the speech, the Reverend Bevel has already won over the emotional mourners with his powerful delivery. However, he proceeds to place their sympathy at risk by proposing that their beloved Dr King is not *really* their leader:

"The Reverend: There's a false rumour around that our leader is dead. *Our* leader is not dead.

The People: No!

(They know King's *spirit* lives on – half the speeches have said that already.)

The Reverend: *That's a false* rumour.

The People: Yes! False! Sho' nuff. *Tell* it!

The Reverend: Martin Luther is not...

(Yes, they know, not dead: this is a form in which expectations are usually satisfied. The crowd arrives at each point *with* the speaker – but the real artist takes chances, creates suspense, breaks the rhythms deliberately; a snag that makes the resumed onward flow the more satisfying.)

The Reverend:... Martin Luther King is not our *leader*!

The People: No!

(The form makes them say it, but with hesitancy. They will trust the Reverend some distance; but what does he mean?)

The Reverend: *Our* leader...

The People: Yes?

The Reverend:... is the man...

The People: *What* man? Who? Who?

(Is it the Reverend Abernathy [another Civil Rights leader]? Is he already trying to supplant King? The trust is almost fading.)

The Reverend:... our leader is the man who led *Moses* out of *Israel*.

The People: *Thass* the man!

(Resolution: all doubt dispelled; the bridge has been negotiated, leaving them stunned with Bevel's virtuosity.)

The Reverend: *Our* leader is the man who went with Daniel into the lion's den.

The People: Some man! Talk some!

The Reverend: Our leader is the man who walked out of the grave on Easter morning.

The People: Thass the leader!

The Reverend: Our leader never sleeps nor slumbers. He cannot be put in jail. He has never lost a war yet. *Our* leader is still *on the case*.

The People: *That's it! On* the case!

The Reverend: Our leader is not dead. One of his prophets died. We will not stop because of that. Our staff is not a funeral staff. We have friends who are undertakers. We *do business*. We *stay on the case* where our leader is."[1]

And so the preacher wins back his congregation. After almost breaking the bond between himself and the people, he comes back with renewed force to drive his final message home – our *real* leader is the Holy Spirit and the Spirit *cannot* be killed. At the end, the crowd is right behind him. They have been moved – swept along on the rhythm of the sermon. And there *is* a rhythm there, just as in music. The speech ebbs and flows and builds up to a crescendo along a line of repeated phrases just like a talking blues or a rock song or a piece of improvised jazz.

You can find many traces of Christian worship in reggae too. The talking back and forth between the preacher and his congregation, the "righteous" sermons, the use of a limited number of familiar stories (Moses, Daniel, etc.) – all these have been taken over and used in reggae music. For example, Toots and the Maytals borrow the service format quite openly for their concerts. Toots Hibbert performs like a preacher mastering his audience. And many of the group's songs use Biblical themes and build up to a climax just like the Reverend Bevel's sermon. Listen, for example, to the early *Six and Seven Books of Moses* (Island, 1963) or *Pressure Drop* (Trojan, 1969). Toots traces his feeling for music back to his childhood when he sang at Sunday school:

> "I was very small and felt I would like to be a prophet when I was a boy. Sometime I would start to sing and the song would break my heart, y'know? I'd feel so *glorious*, y'know, so *good*. I knew I could be something special when I was singing in Sunday School. Now, y'know, my heart is my church and I'm feeling the way I used to feel when I was a boy every day... Musicians do the work of God... when they sing about something that comes from way down here, something that's real. Godliness, uprightness, loving kindness, y'know? Then he becomes a prophet of God."[2]

The story of Moses leading the "suffering Israelites" out of slavery in Egypt is a particular favourite with reggae artists and audiences. It expresses the dream of black people in the New World – that one day they will be free enough to find the Promised Land again. In 1969, Desmond Dekker made a record entitled *Israelites* which was a smash hit in both Jamaica and Great Britain. But it's not just the lyrics themselves which have been influenced by the Bible. As we shall see, one branch of reggae music called the "talk over" is very close indeed to the non-conformist Church sermon. It shares the same pattern of repeated phrases varied subtly each time. There is the same emphasis on the refrain and on the righteous feel of the sermon. And we also find in talk over the same close relationship between the audience and the performer – the same level of feedback from the crowd.

The non-conformist Churches are still very popular in Jamaica, though since the 1930s Pentecostalism has tended to take over from the Baptist faith. And Pentecostal worship is even less restrained. During the services, members of the congregation sometimes go into trances, possessed by the Holy Spirit. In this respect, Pentecostalism has much in common with African cults like *Cumina*. In fact, the African and Christian forms of worship are sometimes so close that some Jamaican cults combine the two. Of these, *Pukkumina* (or "pocomania" – literally "a little madness") is the most African. Revival cults, on the other hand, mix African religious beliefs and rituals together with Christian ones in fairly equal proportions. All these cults have certain common features. There is dancing and drumming and a breathing exercise known as trumping which helps the worshippers go into trances. As the drumming gets faster and faster, the dancers begin what is known as "trumping in the spirit" – writhing on the ground and "speaking in tongues" (sometimes, apparently, in ancient African languages).

All these musical and religious traditions have influenced reggae. But there is another religious movement on the island which is quite different from either the Christian or the African: this is the cult of Rastafari.

Its importance for reggae music is so great that we must deal with it separately.

Chapter Six

The Rastafarians

> "I hear the words of the Rastaman say
> Babylon you throne gone down, gone down,
> Babylon you throne gone down.
> I say fly away home to Zion
> Fly away home.
> One bright morning when my work is over
> Man will fly away home."
>
> *(The Wailers,* Rastaman Chant*)*

The first Rastafarians appeared after Haile Selassie became Emperor of Ethiopia in 1930. The crowning of a black king was greeted enthusiastically throughout the Caribbean. And when in 1935 the Italian fascist dictator Mussolini invaded Ethiopia, there was a tremendous surge of popular support in the West Indies for Selassie and the Ethiopian people. But it was in Jamaica that support for Selassie was most extreme. Soon after Selassie's coronation, three black preachers – Leonard Howell, Joseph Hibbert and Archibald Dunkley – began proclaiming that Selassie was more than just a black hero. For these men and their followers, the Emperor was nothing less than the Living God.

The Rastafarians quoted Biblical prophecies to justify this claim. Selassie numbered among his many official titles, Prince Ras Tafari, the Negus, Lord of Lords and the Conquering Lion of the Tribe of Judah. He was also directly descended from the Old Testament King Solomon.

One of the people who paved the way for the Rastas was Marcus Garvey. Garvey was a Jamaican prophet and one of the first people to encourage black people to be proud of their race and culture. In his writing and speeches, he didn't present Africa as a dark "primitive" continent as the Haitian Griots had done. Instead he stressed the achievements of the ancient African civilisations. He maintained, for instance, that the ancient Ethiopians had been the first to invent reading and writing.

Garvey emigrated to the States in 1914, where he founded the Universal Negro Improvement Association (UNIA). His vision was to bring all black people throughout the world together. And he began pressing for the repatriation of all the descendants of African slaves. This was the origin of the Back to Africa movement which is still supported by some reggae artists. Garvey went on to set up a steamship company called the Black Star Line in order to promote trade with Africa. He was later accused of defrauding the shareholders of this company and was eventually deported from the United States.

Though Garvey died in poverty in London in 1940, he had attracted a large following in black communities throughout the world. And in Jamaica, where he had once been imprisoned, he was eventually made a national hero. Many reggae songs pay homage to Marcus Garvey and proclaim the ideals of the Back to Africa movement. For example, Burning Spear produced a record entitled *Marcus Garvey* in 1975. And in the following year, Big Youth repeated Garvey's prophecies over the slow, heavy dub version of Burning Spear's original recording on a track entitled *Marcus Garvey Dread*.

The myth of the Black Star Line taking black Jamaicans "back" to Ethiopia also remains powerful on the island, even though the original slaves didn't come from Ethiopia at all. In 1977 Fred Locks, a Rastafarian, recorded a reggae song called *Black Star Liners* which dealt with the prophecy that one day Garvey's ships would glide into the harbour at Port Royal to deliver the "suffering black Israelites" out of "Babylon":

> "I can see them coming
> I can see the Idrens [Rasta men and women] running,
> I can hear the elders saying
> These are the days for which we've been praying.
> Seven miles of Black Star liners
> Coming into the harbour."

But it was Marcus Garvey's teachings about a future African king which had the greatest effect on the Rastafarian movement. He urged his followers to "Look to Africa for the crowning of a black king for He shall be the Redeemer". When Selassie was crowned, Garvey's words were remembered. And the Rastafarians proclaimed the Ethiopian Emperor as the new black Messiah.

Over the years, the Rastas developed their own beliefs and rituals. Some grew "dreadlocks" and used Biblical passages to explain why they refused to cut their hair. Many of these "locksmen" smoked the illegal *ganja* (marijuana) plant as a holy sacrament. Again, they linked *ganja* to the "holy herb" which is mentioned in the Bible. For years, the locksmen lived in the poorest parts of West Kingston. They were treated as outcasts, and were either hounded or ignored by the authorities. And then in 1963 and 1965 when isolated incidents of violence involving a few Rastas took place, the Jamaican press and radio condemned the movement outright. All Rastas were labelled as dangerous and violent madmen. In fact nothing could be further from the truth.

Most Jamaican Rastafarians are peaceful people who make a meagre living as artists, fishermen or craftsmen or live off the land in the secluded rural areas. Many refuse to pay taxes or to work for the competitive commercial world which they call "Babylon". Instead they look towards "Zion" – black Africa. Many Rasta men and women refuse to get married and prefer just to live together. But beyond this, it is difficult to say how many beliefs the Rastas hold in common.

Some Rastas work in conventional jobs, others drop out totally. Some smoke *ganja*, others don't. Some believe passionately in going back to Africa while others, particularly the younger locksmen, argue that the first priority is to "deal with Babylon" (that is, to change conditions in the countries they are living in now). One young Rasta living in England (where the cult has a large following) put it like this:

"England is where the truth about I and I lies, so we have to find the truth here before we go back to Africa."[1]

Though many Rastas don't grow dreadlocks, it has nevertheless generally been the locksmen – the most militant and socially outcast Rastafarians – who have had most effect on reggae. These are the Rastas who have given the musicians and many black reggae fans their style. In most places where "heavy" ("roots") reggae is played in Britain or Jamaica, you will see the "locks" or the shorter "natty" (knotty) styles worn by young black reggae fans. And you will also see the red, green and gold colours of the Ethiopian flag, or the red, green and black of Marcus Garvey's UNIA worn on jackets, T-shirts or tams. Rather as the Cuban woman wore her Shango beads as a secret sign of her devotion to the African God, the Rastas wear the Ethiopian colours for Africa. They wear them in much the same way as a Christian might wear a crucifix for Christ.

The recent growth of the Rasta cult is greeted with suspicion by some believers. They believe that there are now many "false Rastas" who wear the Rasta uniform but ignore the teachings about peace and love. Some "false Rastas" have been known to resort to crime and violence:

"They are smashing the Father around. The ones who go around making violence and cheating... They think it's a fashion, you see, but Rasta is not fashion. A Rasta is one who deals in the undefiled truth. Rasta is pureness."[2]

As far as the Rastas are concerned, the only violence they will use is verbal violence. They will denounce the evils of Babylon. They will even seek to draw down God's wrath on the whole "wicked system" but they will not use physical force to achieve their ends. This would be beneath their dignity.

The word Rastafarian refers to a number of different groups, beliefs and attitudes, but they all share a common interest in Ethiopia and the African roots. There are no official Rasta leaders, priests or churches. One Rasta has explained why these aren't considered necessary: "We don't have to go to church because we are churches within ourselves." But the looseness of the Rasta creed is also its strength. It's only by being so flexible and tolerant of individual differences that the cult has brought together so many Jamaicans with so many conflicting opinions. An example of this flexibility working out in practice is the "reasoning", where the locksmen meet to debate points of faith. In many ways, the reasoning sets the whole tone of the Rasta movement. Joe Owens, a Jesuit priest who has lived amongst the Rastas for many years, described a reasoning in an interview for the BBC:

> " ... a reasoning is where it would be anywhere from two up to ... a couple of dozen brethren just sit down, usually over a pipe full of ganja, and just one after another ... express their thoughts in a very poetic and fantastic fashion about whatever is the topic at hand. And it's a very free-flowing type of thing and it can go on for hours non-stop ... Someone will say something and someone else will respond along a slightly different line."[3]

As Owens says, the use of language during reasonings is often poetic – highly imaginative and rich in images drawn from the Bible. The Rastas can draw lessons from the most ordinary events. For example, Michael Thomas tells a story about a Rasta recluse called Cunchyman who "captured" an axe used for cutting wood and hung it on his wall. In this way, Cunchyman claimed that he had conquered the tyranny of work.[4]

The Rastas show the same sensitivity to language in the way they refer to themselves as "I and I". They do this to show that they are not alone: that God, whom they call Jah, is living within them. The phrase is also meant to express the Rastas' feeling of oneness – their sense of solidarity as a group. ("I and I" can be used to mean "we" when one Rasta is speaking for other "idren".) They also add the letter "I" to many other words (e.g., "iternal" instead of "eternal") and many of their own words begin with the letter "I" (e.g., "ital" meaning "wholesome" as in "ital food").

The Rastas stress the importance of personal experience. Each Rasta can make decisions according to his or her own conscience though the Bible always serves as the final reference point. A young British Rasta explains how a highly personal point of view can exist side by side with Biblical teachings:

> "This Bible has the truth but it's locked away from I and I because we were taken away from Africa. But the truth is in I and I as well so it's like a jigsaw puzzle and when you find the right bits it all fits together."[5]

Once again, the value placed upon the individual has helped the cult to survive and flourish. Finally, even the death of Selassie in 1978 hasn't affected the movement's power. Ras Tafari may be physically dead, but as one young Rasta put it: "He lives on in I and I".[6]

It's been estimated that there are now (1979) at least 75,000 Rastafarians in Jamaica. And it seems likely that the cult will continue to grow in Jamaica and England as long as black people remain obviously poorer, less privileged and less likely to get jobs than other racial groups in those countries.

The roots of reggae: Rastafarian and Burru Music

> "Give me back me language and me culture,
> Give me back me language and me culture.
> Dey push dem from out of Africa
> My poor father he was a witch-doctor.
> Dey say he was a damn fool
> And now dey have to push him in school.
> Sing it children!
> Give me back me language and me culture."
> *(Count Ossie and the Mystic Revelations of*
> *Rastafari)*

Reggae music has played an important part in spreading the Rastafarian faith. At the large Rastafarian gatherings called *grounations* or *nyahbingis*, Rastafarian music can be heard constantly. But though the Rastas have contributed greatly to reggae's development, true Rastafarian music is *not* reggae: there are no electric instruments or guitars. Instead, it consists basically of drumming. But its influence on popular music in Jamaica is so strong that it qualifies as another of reggae's many roots.

In the early days, the Rastafarians had no music of their own.

They merely adapted the music of the Revivalist and Pukkumina cults. This consisted of singing and drumming although the rhythms were basically European. Christian hymn tunes were also "captured" and given new Rastafarian lyrics. Gradually the Rastas became more and more aware of the importance of their African roots. They became dissatisfied with the European bias of the music they were playing. So they began searching for African musical traditions on the island. They found one type of music which suited their needs. This was the music of the Burru men.

The Burru men had been on the island for centuries. Their drumming had been the only kind of music officially tolerated on the plantations because it had been used to set the pace at which the slaves worked. When the plantation system began to decline, the Burru men flocked to the Kingston slums where they survived by doing casual work or "scuffling" (scratching a living as best they could). But from September through to December, they spent their time playing the *burra* drums and practising the songs they would sing publicly at Christmas-time.

The Burrus were considered disreputable even by some of their neighbours in the ghetto. Verena Reckford, a Jamaican writer, remembers how she was ordered by her grandmother to stay away from "them damn Burru men":

> "The time I was supposed to spend avoiding Silverwood Alley was spent peeping through nail holes in the dirty zinc fence, at the Burru men playing their drums around a fire, singing and cursing badwords all the time.
>
> To my child's soul, Burru music was the sweetest music ever heard. I could not resist it. If when I was passing, the drums were momentarily silent, I would dally hoping for them to start again, so I could watch the animated faces and bodies, the nimble hands of those unkept Burru men."[7]

It seems the old lady's fears for the safety of her granddaughter were linked to her sense of shame in her African origins. The Burru men looked "wild" and their songs sounded "uncivilised". (In fact, they were based, yet again, in the old insult and praise song traditions of West Africa.) But the grandmother's wariness about the bearded Burru men might have had another cause. For they didn't only play their drums at Christmas-time. They also held a special dance called the Burra to welcome discharged prisoners back into the community.

Like Trinidad's panmen, the Burru drummers had to use whatever materials were at hand to make their instruments. Barrels, paint tins and hollowed out tree trunks were made into drums. And further percussion was supplied by home-made scrapers, "shakkas" (maraccas) and rumba boxes. Sometimes, the Burru men used primitive wind instruments called *saxas*. These were made by stretching cellophane across the mouth of a broken bottle. By singing into the cellophane, the Burru men produced a sound rather like a "kazoo", or a paper and comb.

As soon as the locksmen arrived in Kingston, they came into contact with the Burrus. The two groups had much in common. Both were treated as criminals and social outcasts by the respectable sections of the community. And both were determined to keep the African part of their culture alive. So the Burrus gave the locksmen their music, and the Rastas gave the Burru men their creed. By the late 1930s, the Burrus had more or less merged with the Rastafarians, though a few Burru groups do still exist on the island.

The Rastas began to modify the Burru traditions – adding their own ideas and themes. But the music stayed underground. And to most Jamaican ears it continued to sound sinister and anti-social. The locksmen were often persecuted for their strange appearance. As many were sent to prison for smoking ganja, the anti-social image tended to stick. Soon the Rastas replaced the Burra dance with the *Nyahbingi*, which meant "Death to white oppressors and their black allies". But as the years went by, the language the Rastas used became less violent. By the late 1940s, the Nyahbingi dance was extended until it became a kind of convention where Rastas from all over the island could meet for several days. They would debate the Scriptures, smoke ganja, play the drums, chant and dance. The Nyahbingi is now no longer considered by most Rastas as an actual incitement to physical violence. It probably never was. Like Carl Brouard's poem about the human skulls, the word "Nyahbingi" was designed to shock – to inspire "dread". Now the word means simply "Death to evil forces". According to one Rasta elder: "When we use the Nyahbingi any part of the earth the wicked is, him have to move."[8]

Meanwhile, the Rastafarian drummers were developing their own style using the Burru tradition. They kept the three Burru drums – the bass, "funde" and repeater – but these were now called the *akete* drums. They are all covered with goat-skin. The large bass is still made of barrel staves. It has a low pitch and the drummers strike the skin with a padded stick (often a tennis ball serves as the necessary padding). The *funde* is longer and narrower than the bass, and has an alto pitch. This is played with the palms of the hands. The *repeater* has a soprano pitch and is played with the finger-tips. It takes a great deal of skill to produce the complex repeater melodies. But it's the repeater which gives tension and excitement to Rastafarian music.

As with the music of West Africa, there are two types of Rasta drumming: one for religious and one for non-religious songs. Both types have their own sets of "ridims" (drumming patterns). The religious songs are called "churchical" and the ridims are slow and ponderous. Listen, for instance, to the Wailers' *Rastaman Chant*, which is based on a churchical ridim. The other type of music is called "heartical" and refers to songs which carry social commentary. Here the drumming is faster and lighter.

Rastafarian music was developed mainly for churchical gatherings. But it does serve other purposes too. One Rastafarian explained how it helped him deal with his "downpression" (which might be defined as a cross between feeling *de*pressed and *op*pressed):

> "Suppose for argument sake, I come home one evening and I really feel downpressed. Like I don't make no scufflings all day. I come home and instead of beatin' I wife or roughing up I children I tek out I drum and start a little ridim, y'know. Before yuh know what happen the whole yard is wid I. Yuh no see it? Next thing you know the man mind come off him worries so much so sometimes I get a little insight into how fi [to] tackle me problems next day."[9]

Rastafarian drumming ridims have also influenced both ska and reggae music. Early ska was choppy, uptempo dance music. And it was partly influenced by the non-religious Rasta music – the light heartical ridims. As the years went by, many younger reggae musicians and singers took up the religious ideals of the Rastafarian cult. Their music became heavier, slower and more serious. And from that time on, the influence of the churchical ridims of Rastafarian drumming began to be heard in reggae music.

But there were also direct links between reggae and Rastafarian music. Count Ossie, a Rastafarian drummer who died in 1976, was a kind of living bridge between Rasta music and early ska. Ossie not only helped to develop Rastafarian music. He also brought together many of the original ska musicians.

Ossie began his musical career as a drummer in a Boys' Brigade band. As a young man, he began mixing with the locksmen who were then living in camps in and around Kingston. He was particularly drawn to Burru drumming. But, as he didn't have his own set of drums, he spent every spare moment practising on an old paint tin. By the late 1940s, the large camps were filled with the sound of the drums. Ossie's camp at Adastra Road became an essential port of call for Rastafarian musicians, and he soon began to collect around himself an impressive band.

Anyone who wished to "talk" in music with Ossie and the others was free to come along and join in one of Ossie's long, open jamming sessions. Though no recordings of these original sessions have survived, the music broke new ground and was to prove extremely influential: "At that time we wasn't really checking fe recording. We were only into the music, letting it go free as it come to us."[10]

Amongst Ossie's regular visitors were a number of Rastafarian musicians who were also drawn towards the popular black American sounds – jazz and rhythm and blues (r&b). They wanted to combine all these to make a completely new sound. Many of this particular group played brass instruments. There was "Bra" and Bunny Gaynair, Roland Alphonso, Tommy McCook, Cedric Brooks and "Little G" McNair on saxophone playing alongside Viv Hall, the trumpeter, and the trombonists Don Drummond and Rico Rodriguez. Rico now fronts a reggae band in Britain. But he still remembers how Ossie's drumming provided the perfect backing for his long, jazz-influenced trombone solos:

> "When you play music wid Ossie you kinda *create* music more . . . You see, when you don't hear no chords is like you 'ave a wider scope fe development."[11]

All these musicians played as session men (studio musicians) on the early ska recordings from 1959 onwards. And many of them had fallen under the influence of the same music teacher when they attended the Alpha Reformatory as boys. McCook, Rodriguez, Drummond, Alphonso and a number of other instrumentalists (including the guitarist Ernest Wranglin, who had also jammed with Ossie) joined forces to form a band called The Skatalites. The Skatalites were *the* ska band. Throughout the early 1960s, they produced that unmistakable mixture of driving offbeat rhythms and lonely sounding horns which became known as ska. The group's most successful recording, *The Guns of Navarone*, was named after a Hollywood film. But many of their numbers paid tribute to the Rastafarian movement.

Don Drummond was the driving force behind the group and arguably its most talented musician. At the beginning of the ska era, he built up a formidable reputation as a soloist, only to die tragically a few years later in a mental hospital. Many of his compositions show a Rastafarian influence (e.g., *Father East*, *Addis Ababa* and *Tribute to Marcus Garvey*). But the Skatalites made an impact on ska which went beyond those recordings openly credited to the group.

At this early stage, when the Jamaican record industry was just beginning, there were very few legal restrictions governing record production. Musicians rarely signed contracts with recording companies. As a result, the members of the Skatalites jammed together in a variety of combinations on scores of ska hits. It was standard practice for a group (usually a trio) of vocalists to arrive at the studio. After a swift audition, they would do a straight "one-off" recording of their song. The instrumental backing would be supplied by those musicians who could be quickly contacted. And more often than not, the group would include at least one of the Skatalites. It's because of the open sessions scene in Jamaica that the weird rambling solos of Drummond and Rodriguez can be heard weaving their way through so many records of the period. To complicate matters further, individual members of the Skatalites made solo recordings. And the group also recorded under different names – sometimes as Don Drummond's group or Roland Alphonso's group and sometimes as Tommy McCook's group, the Supersonics.

Almost singlehandedly, the Skatalites were inventing the ska sound on the stages and in the studios of Jamaica. And at least part of the Skatalites' unique style can be traced back to those legendary sessions at Adastra Road with Count Ossie and his Rastafarian drummers. Count Ossie even contributed directly to the ska sound in the early days. He acted as musical adviser and arranger to the Folkes Brothers when they made their classic recording *O Carolina!*. However, Ossie soon became disillusioned with the cut-throat record business. He went back to playing pure Rasta rhythms with his own group, the Mystic Revelations of Rastafari. But his influence on Jamaican pop music can still be heard in reggae. In fact, though, as we shall see, the ska lyrics were generally far from what the Rastas would call "churchical", you can hear Rastafarian themes in the words of many ska numbers.

Even Prince Buster, who produced some of the wittiest, lewdest and most ungodly ska records, often used Rastafarian language in his songs. For instance, in *Free Love* he asks his followers to "act true and to speak true", "to learn to love one another", advising any would-be trouble-makers that "truth is our best weapon" and that "our unity will conquer". The record ends with Buster resenting the fact that the African names of his ancestors have been forgotten in Jamaica and replaced by European ones:

> "With a John on my name and a Tom on my name,
> Mr Campbell on my name, Mr Jones on my name,
> And you tell me that I'm free.
> I must have names like Kenyatta.
> Names like Umbuttu, names like Odinge.
> Got to have our names back,
> Gotta go back where we're from,
> And build homes for each other,
> And grow food for each other.
> Our unity will conquer. Free Love."

If this sounds familiar, just turn back a few pages and look again at the words of the Count Ossie song. For Prince Buster's plea for black Jamaicans to rediscover their African roots is exactly the same as Count Ossie's lament in his song, *Give me back me language and me culture*.

Chapter Seven

The roots of reggae: black American music

We've seen how the Rastafarian rhythms run right through the heart of reggae music. But the early ska musicians were just as strongly influenced by modern jazz and black American r&b. And the first time Jamaicans really came into contact with popular black American music was during the Second World War.

Many black American sailors were stationed on the island. And they brought their own musical tastes and record collections to Jamaica. Soon these jazz and blues records were passing into local hands. And before long, a thriving second-hand record trade had sprung up. Throughout the 1950s interest in black American music was fuelled by American radio – particularly by the small r&b stations situated in and around Miami. On a clear day these broadcasts could be picked up fairly easily even on a battered transistor. And in West Kingston, the r&b produced in New Orleans in the southern part of the US became something of a craze amongst those rich enough or lucky enough to have access to a radio.

Fats Domino, Amos Milburn, Louis Jordan and Roy Brown were particular favourites. The relaxed, loping style of their music seemed to cater to the West Indian taste for unhurried rhythms. In fact, the r&b produced in the southern states of American tended to be much less frantic than the music coming out of the black ghettoes in the north. The southern stuff almost had a Caribbean tinge. In Professor Longhair's rumba-like concoctions, for instance, you can hear influences which never crossed the Mason-Dixon line (the boundary between the northern states and the south). And the characteristic *shuffle* rhythms were there in all the New Orleans r&b.

As the years passed, the demand for black Amerian r&b in Jamaica grew stronger. But there were no local groups who could play the music competently. So large mobile discotheques called "sound systems" were set up to supply the need. The sound systems played imported r&b records at large dances which were held in hired halls or out in the open in the slum yards. The music had to be heavily amplified at these venues if it was to convey the right sense of conviction. And if people were to dance they had to hear the bass, which carried the important "shuffle" rhythm. So the systems got bigger, louder and "heavier". Junior Lincoln, a Jamaican record producer, explains:

> "A sound system is just like what you call a disco. But the only thing is, it is not as sophisticated as a disco set. The amplifiers are huge, well now amplifiers are as big as 2,000 watts. They emphasise a lot on the bass. And they play sometimes twenty or twenty-four inch speakers. So it really thump, y'know. The bass line is really heavy. You've never heard anything so heavy in all your life."[1]

These "blues dances" became a regular feature of ghetto life on the island. Stalls would be set up selling fruit, drink and traditional Jamaican dishes like rice and peas and "curry goat" (curried mutton). And the people would sway for hours to the New Orleans sound clutching their partners and a bottle of Red Stripe beer.

And presiding over the whole affair, mounted on a stage behind the record decks, would sit the all-important disc-jockey. The djs – men like Duke Reid, Sir Coxsone and Prince Buster were, as their names suggest, larger-than-life characters – performers in their own right. Like Trinidad's boastful calypsonians they often played with images of violence, presenting themselves in a jokey but nonetheless menacing fashion as criminals, gangsters and legendary bad men. For instance Duke Reid, who ran one of the most successful of the early sound systems, would preside over blues dances dressed in a long ermine cloak with a pair of Colt 45s in cowboy holsters, a cartridge belt strapped across his ample chest and a loaded shotgun slung over his shoulder, with an enormous gilt crown perched on top of his head.

However, behind all the clowning and the fun, the sound systems were a very serious business. There was money to be made here if enough people could be persuaded to buy the entrance tickets. And the scene soon became intensely competitive as rival djs vied for the crowd's affections. Each system had its own retinue of paid helpers (djs, roadies, engineers and bouncers) as well as an army of loyal supporters. And when, as often happened, two systems were booked to play the same hall, the tension between the two groups would build up through the night. Each system would try to "blow" the other off the stage with rawer and rougher r&b sounds. By midnight the dances would sometimes end abruptly in a full-scale battle just like the steelband dances in Trinidad during the 1950s. And it's rumoured that at such times, at the dances where Reid's system was playing, the Duke himself would restore order by casually lifting the shotgun off his shoulder and firing just above the heads of the brawling mob.

Part of the rivalry between the systems centred on the records themselves. Lee "Scratch" Perry (nicknamed the "Upsetter") remembers how each system tried to win over the crowds by playing the pick of the US imports. Perry began his career in the record business as a "gofer" ("go for" – a messenger boy) for Clement Dodd's Downbeat system. And in the early days, the undisputed "boss sound" was Duke Reid's:

> "Start time we was definitely the smallest of the systems. Duke had some big bad guys operating for him. So my job was to fight down this ... go out and find the best sound. We go out and find them and really upset Duke and them others. It come up we start to have top record all the while and sometime we meet other systems in a club, slug it out toe for toe. Soon we a top shape."[2]

The crowds demanded newer and newer sounds and each system would send off a team of "scouts" to mainland America to search out the cream of the recent r&b releases. The systems looked upon these records as exclusively their own. To ensure that no other system could get hold of these "sides", they scratched off the labels or stuck on new ones to mislead the competition. Occasionally even more devious tactics were tried. Lee Perry describes one trick he played on his arch-rival:

> "One time we put it about that so and so have some real dread sides. Fire sides on a white label. And Duke [Reid] *run* to the man fe buy them. Such a hurry him didn't even play fe check them. And they all old stuff, duds!"[3]

Ska and the early Jamaican record industry

> Bunny Lee: The heat is on.
> Lee Perry: You can say that again. Then how business go?
> Bunny Lee: Can't be worse. I good fe bankrupt any moment now.
> Lee Perry: Then you kyaan [can't] get a loan?
> Bunny Lee: Wha! Any bank you check now all you can hear is the bank manager amoan and the teller them agroan.
> Lee Perry: Man! It look like them a kill us softly..."
> *(Lee Perry and Bunny Lee,* Laberish)

By the late 1950s, the stream of r&b imports from the States was beginning to dry up and three sound systems men – Duke Reid,

Prince Buster and Sir Coxsone Dodd – began to produce their own primitive r&b recordings using local session musicians. To begin with, these records were called *rudie blues*. They were definitely not for public sale. Like the r&b imports, they remained the cherished possession of the sound system owners who had financed the recording. Most of these early rhythm and blues tracks were purely instrumental cover versions of old r&b favourites or original compositions in the New Orleans style. The vocal accompaniment was added live by the djs themselves at the blues dances. They would "scat" or "toast" (improvise lyrics) over the record as it played. And they tended to stick to a few simple slogans – encouraging the dancers with cries like "Work it! Work it!" "Move it up!" or just screeching out a repertoire of stock phrases, some of which derived from non-conformist Church worship: "Good God Almighty!" Eventually, the djs' vocal "toasts" were themselves recorded. And in time, the improvising dj style gave rise to two important types of reggae music – *talk over* and *dub*.

But even on these early "rudie blues" recordings, the original r&b sound had been modified by the Jamaican session musicians. The shuffle rhythms of New Orleans remained, but they became somehow flattened out – the beats became more *even* than in r&b. And all the instruments seemed to linger for a longer space of time on the off beat. By 1961 the Jamaican rhythms could be easily distinguished from the r&b sound and a new musical form emerged. Soon this new form of pop music, unique to Jamaica, had its own name – ska. No one knows exactly why ska developed in the way it did, but it seems likely that Jamaican musicians brought their own traditions to American music. And as we've seen, an important part of those Jamaican traditions was the drumming of the Rastafarian cult. The transition from the "second hand" rudie blues to the original sound of ska was partly brought about through the influence of Rasta and Burru drumming.

Count Ossie himself was involved for a time in the sound system scene which gave birth to both ska and the Jamaican record industry. During the mid 1950s, Ossie played at the ghetto blues dances. At midnight the sound system would pack up and the Rastafarian drummers would settle down to play righteous music and heartical songs till dawn came and the dancers staggered home. Even at the height of the r&b craze in Jamaica, the Rastafarian ridims were still popular in downtown Kingston. And those ridims played their part in inflecting (changing the character and accent of) black American music. According to Joe Higgs, a reggae veteran whose career as a singer goes back to the 1950s, ska was "more to the African touch . . . more relevant to the drums" than r&b.[4]

During the early 1960s, the most successful ska sound system was run by Prince Buster. Buster was an ex-boxer who began his career in the record business – like so many other Jamaican producers and recording engineers – working for a big sound system. He started as a bouncer for Duke Reid, but was soon promoted to dj. After buying a record shop on Orange Street – Kingston's Tin Pan Alley – he set up his own sound system and started making his own records. In 1956 he made *Little Honey* and later *Wash Wash* and *Lion of Judah*. In *They Got to Go*, he criticised the big systems, run at that time by older men, who tended to support American music at the expense of local ska.

But the success of Buster's sound soon established ska as the most popular music in Jamaica. Buster went on to develop his own distinctive vocal style based on the old dj "toasts". Over a backing of raucous horns, driving shuffle drums and a thumping bass, Prince Buster would brag about his prowess as a fighter and a lover.

On *The Ten Commandments*, for instance, he lays down the law for "his woman" in a blustering manner which recalls the swaggering male chauvinist style of Trinidad's Mighty Sparrow:

> "Remember to kiss and caress me, honour and obey me
> In my every whim and fancy, seven days a week,
> And twice on Sunday."

On *Earthquake*, he throws down a challenge to anyone on Orange Street – "the street with a the beat" – who wishes to challenge his supremacy:

> "Man stand up and fight if you're right!
> Earthquake on Orange Street!"

And finally, on *Al Capone*, Buster assumes the role of the most famous gangster of them all. Against a background of screeching tyres and sporadic bursts of machine-gun fire, he issues the following warning:

> "Don't call me Scarface. My name is
> Kerpown-C-A-P-O-N-E-Kerpown!"

For Buster, ska was always nothing more than good music to get up and dance to. And the kind of dancing associated with ska was strongly rooted in Jamaican folk traditions. In Buster's own words:

> "The proper dance in Jamaica to ska music was the bebop dance. Push and spin and natural Jamaican things like flashing [snapping] the fingers and pickup moves from Pocomania and mento."[5]

In fact, Prince Buster sometimes drew directly on these Jamaican folk traditions. On one of his early records called *Ghost Dance* he recreates the atmosphere of a Cumina or Pocomania gathering. He summons up "spirits", sighs and begins "trumping" like a worshipper in the throes of possession, whilst in the background a mournful trombone flits in and out of earshot like a restless ghost.

But not all ska had such an obviously Jamaican flavour. Many records were produced with the mainstream market in mind. Owen Grey's *Darling Patricia*, Jackie Edward's *Tell me Darling* and Jackie Opel's *Cry me a River* – all ska or pre-ska hits – fall into this category. They were uptempo ballads with the strong romantic themes which are common to all forms of modern pop music. Millicent (Millie) Small was the first Jamaican artist to break through to an international audience in 1963 with *My Boy Lollipop*. This was a coy love song with toned-down ska rhythms but it entered both the British and American charts.

From the very earliest days, people like Eddie Seaga of Federal Studios attempted to clean up ska and make it acceptable to white audiences abroad. Seaga later became leader of the opposition Jamaica Labour Party. He began promoting Byron Lee and the Dragonaires – a group who tried to graft the ska beat on to familiar Caribbean classics like *Yellow Bird* and *Island in the Sun*. However, the group failed to make a favourable impression at the 1964 New York World's Fair. And on the island itself, the ghetto audiences still preferred to move to the rawer sound of undiluted ska. Apart from Prince Buster, groups like the Skatalites, Justin Hines and the Dominoes, and the Vikings (who backed the early Wailers and the Maytals) were very popular during this period.

Throughout the early 1960s the record industry continued to thrive. Every day new talent would be discovered. New singers would turn up at the crowded Orange Street record shops armed with a sheet of lyrics and a lot of nerve. Singers presenting themselves in this way would have to suffer a long, humiliating wait before the producers would listen to their compositions. Often the producer would dismiss them before he even heard the first line of the song if he wasn't in the right mood or the singer's face didn't fit. This is how Jimmy Cliff, who later had big hits with songs like *Wonderful World, Beautiful People* and *You Can Get it if You Really Want*, began his recording career. Almost as soon as he arrived in Kingston at the age of thirteen, Cliff determined to break into the record business as a singer. After cutting a few exclusive sides for various sound systems, he managed to get a song called *Daisy Got me Crazy* issued in 1962 when he was fourteen years old. Like many other early Jamaican artists, he received no payment. But he went on to write a song called *Dearest Beverley* and set out to convince a local businessman named Leslie Kong that it could be used to promote Kong's record store, which was also called Beverley's. Kong agreed, hired a studio and cut the record, which became a minor hit. Afterwards, Kong remained in the record business as a highly successful producer till his death in 1971.

Soon producers like Kong began competing with Prince Buster for control of the ska industry. During these years, Lee Scratch Perry, went on working for Sir Coxsone Dodd, who had opened up his own studio – Studio One:

> "From since 59 coming up 60, me start audition in [Dodd's] little shop down Orange Street. Any artist me feel good enough, me say [to Dodd] 'select this one fe session, record him'... Like Toots [Hibbert] come for audition and I the man force Dodd take on Toots... We go to the studio and he give *Six and Seven Books of Moses* and *rip* it up."[6]

Later, the ska beat became properly established and Prince Buster's soon became the "boss sound". Scratch and many of the younger men on the sound system scene joined ranks with Dodd and set out to topple Buster:

> "We young guys would go along and write songs to counteract Buster's sounds – sounds like Delroy Wilson's *I Shall Never Remove* and *Spit in the Sky and It Fall in Your Eye*. And we a killing off Buster backwards."[7]

Today's record business owes much to the early hectic years of ska. Record production is still an intensely competitive and sometimes literally cut-throat business. Many producers carry facial scars won in the pursuit of bigger profits.

Present-day producers, many of whom grew up in the ghettoes to the sound of ska, are also often talented all-rounders just like the old sound system men. For instance, Prince Tony is a successful record producer. Though born in the slums of Princess Street and still only in his early thirties, he has already owned at different times a sound system and two record shops. At the moment, he is in the process of buying his own manufacturing plant. He has produced records by top dj stars like U Roy and Big Youth, managed the reggae group The Gladiators, produced their best-selling album *Trench Town Mix Up*, and personally promoted all these artists and their records throughout Jamaica, Britain and the States.

The producers have usually had to be extremely tough and wily to rise to the top in such a competitive business. Indeed the ruthlessness of some of them is legendary. Young reggae musicians are still sometimes forced to work for a pittance. To give just one example, Barrington Spence, a Jamaican reggae singer, claims to have earned only £15 for his song *High Blood Pressure*, which sold at least 12,000 copies. Resentment over unpaid royalties is so much a part of Jamaica's record scene that it's even been included as a theme in the reggae film *The Harder They Come* (Warner Bros, 1972). In the film, the hero, Ivan O Martin (played by Jimmy Cliff) is paid only twenty dollars for his number one hit, *The Harder They Come*. The young man's frustration with the record business contributes to his decision to take to violent crime – a decision which leads to his death in a hail of police and army bullets in the final reel.

In a lighter vein, the vocal trio, Culture, fell out with their record producer, Joe Gibbs, and his engineer, Errol (ET) Thompson, after releasing a successful LP in 1977. In an interview with the magazine *Black Music*, Joe Hill, the group's lead singer, hurled insults at his former associates alleging all manner of dirty tricks. Finally, he delivered a prophecy in the style of his hit record *Two Sevens Clash*:

> "... until the day when the sun start rises from the West and set in the East, I'll never sing a single line for him no more. And I hereby prophesy and I say: 'Joe Gibbs and engineer name Errol Thompson, one of these days you'll want the tape I *laugh* on ... And you won't get it brothers!'"[8]

In 1974, two reggae producers, Lee Perry and Bunny Lee, produced a comic record called *Laberish*. The two men gossip over a rhythm track and give *their* version of the business rather than that of the artists. They come across as a pair of amiable rogues. Instead of pleading their innocence, they set out to confirm the popular idea of the producer as a pirate. They laugh at their less successful competitors and moan about their finances. Finally, in a stroke of self-directed humour, they accuse the "greedy artists" of bankrupting Niney, a rival record producer:

> "Bunny Lee: Wha' happen to Niney?
> Lee Perry: He got no clothes 'cos him pay him artists 12½per cent royalty."

Producers like Scratch Perry and Clement Dodd, whose careers began with ska, went on to far larger studios producing a much more polished sound. And artists like Jimmy Cliff, the Wailers and the Maytals who started recording at the same time, went on to bigger and better things. But the reggae industry remains as competitive as it ever was. It grew up alongside ska and much of its cut-throat character derives from the sound systems and the early days of

Jamaican popular music. And though the music has changed pace and direction, the basic rhythm still has its roots in the old ska sound. As Buster himself has said:

> "All of reggae music is still basically ska. The strongest sellers still have that good afterbeat."[9]

Chapter Eight

Rocksteady and the rude boy era

"Walking down the road with a pistol in your waist
Johnny you're too bad.
Walking down the road with a ratchet in your waist
Johnny you're too bad.
You're jesta robbing and a stabbing and a looting and a
    shooting
You know you're too bad."

(The Slickers)

Ska continued to dominate the Jamaican pop music scene until the summer of 1966. Then the music suddenly began to slow down to a "stickier", more sinister rhythm. A completely new dance style emerged. Gone were the fast, jerky movements of ska. Instead, a slinkier, cooler dance called the *rocksteady* became popular. According to Sonny Bradshaw, a veteran musician from the ska days, the rocksteady rhythm caught on because it was much "slower and gave [the dancers] more time to do what they wanted to do". In rocksteady, ska's rumbling bass lines became deeper and still more noticeable. The brass was phased out to be replaced by guitar and keyboard set-ups. The main solo instrument of early ska – the trombone – disappeared virtually overnight, although saxophone breaks in the Latin American style were featured on many rocksteady records.

There were also changes in the way the recordings were made and mixed. In the early days, when the sound system operators first began making records, the studio facilities had been very primitive. Usually the music was played by session musicians and the recording was made in one take. Before long, vocal tracks were added too. The instrumentals were recorded on one track of the tape and this was later pressed as a record. But as the industry evolved and became more sophisticated, so too did the recording equipment. Soon it became possible to mix together a number of musical tracks to build up a more complex and interesting sound. At the same time, the engineers experimented by mixing the tracks together on the final tape in different ways. For instance, ska and rocksteady records were mixed differently. In ska, the vocal track had been given prominence, and this is still the case with most forms of modern pop music where the lyrics are considered important. But on the new rocksteady records, the singers' voices tended to be treated like any other instrument. Instead, pride of place was given to the bass guitar.

A new generation of artists and producers was thrown into the spotlight by the rocksteady craze. Alton Ellis produced the first rocksteady record, called simply *Rocksteady*, in 1966. He followed its success with a string of hits including *I'm Just a Guy* and *I'm Still in Love* which dwelt on the themes of love and courtship. Delroy Wilson was the most successful newcomer with hits like *Dancing Mood* and *I'm Not a King*. And there was even an instrumental group called The Soul Vendors who more or less did for rocksteady what the Skatalites had done for ska. The Soul Vendors produced a number of popular dance tunes such as *Ba Ba Boom*, *The Whip* and *Ram Jam*.

All the popular rocksteady numbers mentioned so far were conventional dance tunes, and the lyrics, if any, tended to be fairly predictable. But in 1966, two new words entered the vocabulary of Jamaican pop music to go with the new rhythm. The words were "rude boy", and they referred to a group of youths who hung out on the slum street corners. They were mostly unemployed and had taken to carrying German ratchet knives and hand guns. They could be anything from fourteen to twenty-five years old and came from all over West Kingston. And above all, the rude boys were *angry*. Conditions in West Kingston had hardly improved with the passing years. Rather than buckle under to a life spent doing menial work or no work at all, the rude boys took to the streets and to crime.

There was a certain style to it all. The rudies wore very short green serge trousers, leather or gangster-style suit jackets, and their eyes were often hidden behind moody pairs of shades. If they were "rough, tough" and rich enough, they would ride around on light, stripped-down motor cycles which were covered in chrome. Apart from stealing, scuffling or hustling, the rude boys might spend their time playing an aggressive game of dominoes or "tram hopping" – leaping (sometimes backwards) onto the bars at the rear of the trams as they rattled through the city streets. The point was to be as cool as possible. But sometimes, particularly at the blues dances, the "pressure" would get too much – fights would break out and guns and knives would be drawn. I Roy, a popular talk-over artist, still remembers what it was like when the dreaded rude boys "crashed" a dance:

> "They used to come to open air dances and they buy say six beers one time – Red Stripe beers, bottles with long necks ... A man had three beers in this hand and then three beer [in the other]. And a certain tune play and he's really crazy

about this tune, and he just *crashes* the six bottle. And then people start running all section... It was a sort of style, y'know? Man says 'Why the rude boys passing through the dance last night. Them really *hack* it up, y'know? People had to jump [over the] fence and all them thing there!'"[1]

The rude boy style had been a part of the sound system scene even in the early 1960s: there had then been the "rudie blues". And Roland Alphonso released an early ska record in 1962 which dealt with the rude boys. However, it wasn't until 1966, when the Wailers produced *Rude Boy* for Clement Dodd, that the cult really took off inside Jamaican pop music. The Wailers followed this with a string of minor rudie hits which included *Rule Them Rudie* and the classic *Steppin' Razor*. Other groups and artists soon followed suit, and throughout 1967 the Jamaican charts were filled with rude boy songs. Like the saga boy calypsoes of the late 1940s they tended to glamourise crime and rebellion. *Everybody Rude Now* by Keith McCarthy, *Tougher than Tough* by Derrick Morgan and Dandy Livingstone's *Rudy a Message to You* were all hits during this period.

Not to be outdone, Prince Buster released a string of rudie anthems, including *Too Hot*, in which he presented a rude boy boast in his usual mock-serious manner:

"Rude boys never give up their guns,
No one can tell them what to do.
Pound for pound they say they're ruder than you.
Get out insurance and make up your will
If you want to fight them."

Buster went on poking gentle fun at the rude boys throughout the period in the guise of Judge Dread, a terrifying Ethiopian magistrate. The Judge is determined to clamp down on youths who go around beatin' up black people. On *Judge Dread*, Buster sentences a group of rude boys who can be heard weeping and pleading for mercy in the background ("Order! Order! Rude boys don't cry!") to 500 years and 10,000 lashes. However, in the follow-up, *Barrister Pardon*, Buster relents and, whilst the trombones blare out typical ska riffs, the judge grants them a pardon and throws a party to celebrate their release.

After a time, the rude boy craze died down. But in 1971 there was a revival of interest in the cult sparked off by the release of the soundtrack to the film *The Harder They Come*. This album contained the Slickers' *Johnny Too Bad* and a re-issue of Desmond Dekker's 1967 hit, *Shanty Town (007)*:

"And now rude boys have a wail
Cos them out a jail.
Rude boys cannot fail

> Cos them must get bail.
> Dem a loot, dem a shoot, dem a wail
> In shanty town."

The rude boy style continued to be popular right through the reggae period. Even now, many reggae stars, particularly dj artists, project an image which is reminiscent of the old rudie style. Big Youth and Dillinger have both produced discs which deal with the motorcycle subculture. On *Ace Go Skank*, Big Youth warns any aspiring rude boys: "If ya ride like lightning, ya crash like thunder". And Dillinger's reputation as a reggae star rests largely on his hit *CB 200* which was named after a Honda bike.

In the tough areas of West Kingston, the motorcycle, the gun and ratchet knife are still a way of life for some black youths. The slums can still be a dangerous battleground. The level of political violence in the run-up to the 1976 elections got so high that the Prime Minister declared a State of Emergency. A Gun Court was set up in the centre of Kingston and a law was passed whereby anyone found carrying a gun could be immediately arrested and detained for an indefinite period. Bob Marley himself was wounded by a gunman at the end of the year and an attempt was made on the Prime Minister's life. The situation only began to improve when Claudie Massop and Buckie Marshall, the rude boy gunmen for the two political parties in Kingston's slums, signed a truce and decided to work together to improve local conditions. This move for peace was started largely by the Rastafarians. The shift from violent to peaceful solutions to Jamaica's problems was reflected in the next phase of the island's pop history – reggae.

Chapter Nine

Reggae

"One good thing about music, when it hit you
you feel no pain."
(Bob Marley and the Wailers, Trench Town Rock*)*

Around 1968, the music shifted down another gear, becoming even
slower and "heavier" with an even greater emphasis on the bass. The
new rhythm was certainly there on Toots and the Maytals' hit *Do the
Reggay*. But it can also be heard on a slightly earlier recording
entitled *People Funny Boy*, which had been produced by Lee
"Scratch" Perry. By this time Scratch had left Sir Coxsone Dodd's
Studio One label and was striking out on his own. As far as he
recollects, the idea of the reggae beat came to him as he was walking
past a Pocomania Church:

> " ... See, at them time, me used to go out town and stay late,
> drink some beer, thing like that. And one night me walking
> past a Pocomania church and hear the people inside a wail.
> And me catch the vibration and say, 'Boy! Let's make a
> sound fe catch the vibration of the people!' Them was in the
> spirit and them tune me spiritually. That's where the thing
> come from, 'cos them Poco people getting sweet!"[1]

At the same time, Scratch wanted to break away from the ska and
rocksteady rhythms which he felt were becoming too familiar and
clichéd. Above all, he wanted to produce a sound which would
"upset" his rivals, particularly Sir Coxsone Dodd:

> "'Cos they were doing something same all the way, man. All
> of them a just go 'ska-aska-ska-aska'. And when the people
> hear what I man do them hear a different beat, a waxy beat –
> like you stepping in glue. Them hear a different bass, a rebel
> bass, coming at you like sticking a gun."[2]

The "waxy beat" and "rebel bass" proved a killing combination. And
the reggae rhythms proved so popular that the word "reggae" now
applies to virtually all forms of Jamaican pop. Scratch went on to
produce artists like the Wailers, the Upsetters, U Roy, Junior Murvin
and Max Romeo, and soon became the acknowledged master of
heavy "roots" reggae.

But not all reggae sounded like a gun being placed against the eardrums. The kind of reggae which was most popular in Jamaica at this time was generally lighter and less menacing. The lyrics dealt mainly in the language of love and broken hearts. Singers like Alton Ellis, John Holt, Pat Kelly and Ken Boothe began recording smooth romantic ballads, sometimes with a lush accompaniment of strings and a full orchestra. These were very popular with the slightly older age group. And they also sold outside the usual reggae market. Albums by singers like Holt continue to sell quietly but steadily. For many years, the record industry tended to promote mainstream "commercial" reggae at the expense of the "ethnic" roots product. This was merely an extension of the old policy of diluting Caribbean music for the international audience.

As far as the international record companies were concerned, Jamaica's heavy stuff was too rough and rude for white ears. When Max Romeo's *Wet Dream* began creeping up in the British charts in 1969, the BBC banned it because of its blatantly sexual lyrics. It's therefore hardly surprising that when reggae *did* finally cross over into the international market, it was the commercial product that won through first. *I Can See Clearly Now* by Johnny Nash made a big impact on the British and American charts in 1971. And if the record sounds only remotely related to "roots reggae", that's because Nash, an American singer, had specialised in middle of the road romantic ballads before turning to the new Jamaican rhythm.

But gradually, in Jamaica itself, a new harder type of reggae began to win over the younger audiences. For instance, in 1971, Eric Donaldson won the Jamaica Song Festival with a number called *Cherry Oh Baby*. This was fairly traditional as far as the lyrics were concerned. But the faltering beat and thumping bass line, together with Donaldson's yearning falsetto voice, gave the record an eerie, haunting quality which was difficult to resist. Meanwhile, Toots and the Maytals were transferring more and more complex harmonies from the church to the recording studio. In *Sweet and Dandy* (1969) and *Pressure Drop* (1968), the voices of Toots, Jerry Mathias and Raleigh Gordon weave together in a call and response pattern against the fast, driving rhythm of the backing band to create an effect not unlike that of a Baptist congregation in full swing. And in 1968 the group released one of their most powerful recordings, *54-46 That's my Number*, which was based on Toots' own experiences as a prisoner, when he served a sentence for the possession of ganja in 1966.

However, there was an even more significant development. Many of the younger reggae stars became more and more committed to the social and religious ideals of the Rastafarian cult. Gradually, the

Rasta themes of peace, solidarity and black pride began to work their way into reggae songs. One of the first really successful records to publicise the Rasta creed was *Blood and Fire* by Niney the Observer (who went on to become a record producer and dub master). *Blood and Fire* was produced in a single hectic session at Randy's studio one December night in 1970. Niney could only afford to book the studio for an hour and was forced to race across Kingston to another studio – Dynamic – to pick up some session musicians:

> "We set up ... and record the tune and me take three quarter hour to make the rhythm and voice it. True me never want to sing that tune 'cos I just have the idea but ... I *force* to sing it myself. And I need harmony but there was no one to give harmony. But as we in Randy's half hour I see Buster Brown and Dobby Dobson and Lloyd Charmers and I say 'I need harmony' and them say 'Well, that alright' ..."[3]

Strangely enough, given the conditions under which it was made, *Blood and Fire* turned out to be technically brilliant. It opened up new possibilities for both producers and lyric writers. The bass bubbles along as the lead guitar repeats the same jagged riff over and over again. To a background chorus of "Let it burn/Let it burn/Let it burn, burn, burn" sung in a surprisingly unconcerned, melodious style, Niney himself mutters his ambiguous prayer:

> "Blood, blood, blood, blood and fire.
> Rasta hail pipe.
> Blessed is the pipe that is always light
> In the house of Jah Rastafari.
> Blessed is the weed of the ganja seed
> That keeps breeding the ganja breed.
> Blood and fire, let it burn.
> All weak heart shall leak out and split up
> All righteous shall stand.
> Hail, Rasta, hail and wail
> Hail, Rasta, don't quit.
> Blood, blood, blood, blood and fire.
> Let it burn."

Blood and Fire went on to become a major hit in Jamaica (though typically, Niney claims he was cheated out of his rightful profits by the man who ran the record-pressing plant). The cult of Rastafari had finally surfaced in popular music. But it was left to another man and another group to promote roots reggae and the Rasta message to the world. The man, of course, was Bob Marley and the group were the Wailers.

Bob Marley and the Wailers

Robert Nesta Marley was born in 1945 in the parish of St Ann, deep in rural Jamaica. His father, a retired major in the British army, left the household soon after his son's birth. The boy was brought up by his mother – a local woman. On leaving school at fourteen, the young Marley headed for Kingston where he settled in Trench Town at the family home of Bunny Livingston, who was later to become the Wailers' high harmony singer.

Marley served the usual reggae apprenticeship – hanging around, doing odd jobs, cutting a few forgotten r&b records for a local producer. And then in 1964 he met two men who were to influence his life profoundly – Joe Higgs and Mortimer Planno. Higgs, one half of the Higgs and Wilson recording duo, introduced Marley to harmony and showed him how to arrange his songs. Planno, a much older man, initiated Marley into the mysteries of the Rasta faith: Planno was very highly regarded in Rasta circles. He introduced Marley to Alvin Patterson, a Rasta drummer who taught Marley the importance of "ridim" and time. Planno claims to have foreseen Marley's future success and he regards music as a valuable "weapon for peace" – a means of spreading the Rasta doctrine without bloodshed.

In late 1964, Marley formed a group called the Wailing Rude Boys with himself as singer and guitarist. Bunny Livingston and Peter MacIntosh (Tosh) were signed up as support vocalists. The trio recorded a few tracks for Clement Dodd and then, in 1967, Marley left for America. However, he was soon drawn back to Kingston and the reggae business. In 1968 he joined forces with the Upsetters, Lee Perry's resident studio band, who have backed many of Jamaica's top vocalists as well as laying down some of the strongest rhythm tracks on Scratch's famous dubs. Carly Barrett, the drummer and his brother, Family Man, the bassist, were recruited as the Wailer's backing group. As Family Man puts it:

> "The Wailers was the best vocal group anywhere in Jamaica, and I group [my group] was the best little backing band, so we say, 'Why don't we come together and mash up the world!'"[4]

By this time, the Wailers had discarded their rude boy image. They began wearing the Ethiopian colours and growing the dreadlocks which were to become a trademark of roots reggae. And the lyrics of their songs became increasingly militant and concerned with the issue of social and racial inequality. With Lee Perry, the Wailers recorded some of their strongest, most politically conscious numbers including *Small Ax*, *400 Years*, *Get up, Stand up* and *Trench Town Rock*.

Eventually Marley and the Wailers met Chris Blackwell, who had set up one of the most successful reggae labels – Island Records.

Blackwell, the son of a white Jamaican plantation owner, was an extremely shrewd businessman. He had been one of the first to recognise the potential for growth of ska in the UK where large numbers of West Indian immigrants had come to settle during the 1950s and 1960s. He started in the record business in 1962, when he began promoting and distributing ska records in London's West Indian ghettoes and it was Blackwell who in 1963 scored the first Jamaican hit in Britain with Millie's *My Boy Lollipop*. In 1972, after building up Island into a highly profitable concern, he decided to invest in the Wailers' first LP.

Blackwell broke all the rules as far as reggae producers were concerned. Instead of restricting the group by giving them tight deadlines and low budgets, he allowed them to produce their own kind of music in their own kind of time. There were, of course, good business reasons for all this. By this time, he was interested in developing the "cross-over" (i.e., white) market. But he was far more imaginative than most of the record company executives who had previously tried to promote reggae outside Jamaica. Blackwell realised that the strength of the roots product lay in its un-compromising quality and that the young white rock audience would respond to Marley's "rebel music" in its pure Jamaican form. Instead of trying to tone down the social and political content of the Wailers' lyrics, he went out of his way to underline it. Instead of insisting that the group wear shiny suits and ties, he positively encouraged them to grow their hair and adopt the Rasta image.

But he also realised that, if reggae were ever really to cross over, it would have to be produced, promoted and packaged like any other pop or rock music. Instead of issuing one-off singles, Blackwell concentrated on well-produced stereo LPs aimed at the hi-fi market. He calculated quite correctly that white fans with hi-fi systems were far more likely to add a glossily produced reggae LP to their record collections, than to buy a few imported singles which were expensive and difficult to get hold of.

The Wailers were to be sold to the public. No expense was to be spared – posters, publicity, press releases, television appearances, radio and newspaper interviews, international tours – all these would serve to keep the group in the public eye. So it was that when *Catch A Fire* finally reached the record shops, it benefited both from the rootsy feel of the music and from the sophisticated recording and promotion techniques which Blackwell placed at the group's disposal. The consumer had the best of both worlds – a product which was at one and the same time "polished" and "gritty". The album cover carried a portrait of Marley which emphasised his burning eyes and flying locks in a way which was designed to appeal to the rebellious instincts of the young rock fans. And in the same way, the record itself combined raw roots reggae with a polished studio sound. The original recording was mixed in a Kingston studio by the group themselves. But Blackwell considered it a little too heavy for the white audience, so he re-mixed it in London. He brought Marley's voice forward and toned down the distinctive bass. He also added some flowing rock guitar riffs recorded by local British session men to the original tape.

But the words of the songs were left intact. Many of the numbers originally recorded for Scratch were included on the LP. And the lyrics were completely uncensored:

> "Slave driver the table is turned.
> Catch a fire so you can get burned."

And just in case white listeners unaccustomed to the Jamaican patois missed the point, the lyrics were reprinted on the album sleeve. Throughout the whole LP, Marley, in his unearthly, wailing voice "chants down Babylon" and prophesies destruction for the wicked. The Rasta images of vengeful fire and Babylon falling continued on the Wailers' second LP, *Burning*, which was also released on the Island label. As with Niney's *Blood and Fire*, the LP's title managed to suggest that by burning the ganja weed, the Rastas were merely looking forward to the time when Babylon itself would be consumed in flames sent by God on Judgement Day.

Marley was eventually to emerge as the first reggae superstar, although the Wailers' success caused frictions inside the group. Before the third album, *Natty Dread*, was released in 1974, Tosh and Livingston were refusing to undergo yet another gruelling tour of Britain and the States. Marley changed the line-up for the 1975 tour, hiring musicians and adding a female backing group, the I-Threes. He toured Africa, Europe and North America over the next few years; produced a live album (*Wailers Live*) and three other LPs for Island Records – *Rastaman Vibration*, *Exodus* and *Kaya*, and in his last years, Marley won respect not only in Jamaica but from music critics and fans throughout the world.

But this situation had created new problems for Marley. His fame made him a prime target for politically motivated violence. After the attempt on his life in 1977, he was forced to leave Jamaica for his own safety. Marley's live performances were among the most exciting and compelling in rock music. When Marley raised his hands, shook his shoulder-length locks and began playing *Exodus* on British television's *Top of the Pops* in 1977, it was indeed an historic occasion.

Against a huge painted backdrop of Marcus Garvey and Haile Selassie, Marley sung the song which tells the story of the "movement of the Jah people" from Africa to Jamaica and on towards "Holy Mount Zion". And this in the hallowed studios of the BBC at the heart of the old British Empire!

Other Jamaican artists have benefited from the interest in roots reggae which Marley has stimulated. Groups like the Mighty Diamonds, the Gladiators, Third World, Burning Spear and Culture have all toured outside Jamaica and attracted a large following amongst young white rock fans. Peter Tosh and Bunny Livingston have both gone on to produce successful solo albums, and both artists have refused to stray far from their roots. On *Legalise It* and *Equal Rights*, Tosh showed himself to be just as angry as in the old Wailers days when he wrote songs like *400 Years* and *Get up, Stand up*. And Bunny Livingston's album *Blackheart Man* was a tribute to his fellow Rastas. Records by both ex-Wailers have sold well in Europe and the States. Tosh even overcame his aversion to touring when he visited Britain in 1979. Even Ras Michael and the Sons of Negus, whose music is based on traditional Rasta drumming, have toured Britain and played to white audiences.

All these successes are ultimately due to the larger success of Marley himself. But part of the reason why Marley's music broke through in this way is that his songs are basically melodic. The music always sounds sweet, even when the lyrics include scathing attacks on the colonial system. Like the calypsonians, Marley knew how to drive his message home behind a lilting refrain or a jaunty beat. It's the classic Caribbean package of bitter social commentary wrapped up in a light, refreshing rhythm. In effect, Marley was making the Western world dance to the prophecies of its own destruction.

But by the early 1970s singers and musicians in Jamaica were reviving the old forbidden "ridims" by bringing up the bass and the drums. And they were out to make music which was so "heavy" that the listeners would be left in no doubt as to its real meaning. In the words of Big Youth, the spokesman for the new style: "No more songs about girls..."[5]

Chapter Ten

Dub and talk over

"Me love dub and but I and I don't get involved with it too much. Dub means right and tight, the perfect groove. When Wailers say *dub* this one, dis mean we gonna play it right and tight." *(Bob Marley)*

"You can copyright a song, but you can't copyright a rhythm."

(Dermott Hussey, Jamaican record producer*)*

We have already seen how, in order to get through to the wider audience, the Wailers' LP had to be remixed so that the overall sound was brought into line with the expectations of the white rock audience. Many of the reggae LPs produced with the foreign market in mind are still remixed in this way. For example, some producers speed up the tapes slightly for reggae records destined for the American market, because the American rock and soul audiences who are likely to buy reggae prefer the faster rhythms. However in Jamaica the slower, heavier rhythms continued to be popular and around 1974 reggae began to slow down yet again until it began to sound even more menacing.

The new "dread ridims" were called *rockers*. As with every other shift in Jamaican pop music, the new sound can be traced back to the way the drums and bass guitar were featured on recordings. In rockers, the bass was as heavily amplified as ever and continued to provide the basic background throb – reggae's heartbeat. But the bass patterns also became more complicated and experimental. In some types of heavy reggae (especially in instrumental or "dub" music) the bass takes over the prominent role normally reserved in rock music for the lead guitar. Robbie Shakespeare, a session musician who plays for the studio band The Aggravators, is held largely responsible for the new bass style. The drumming, too, became more complicated in rockers' music and again the change is generally attributed to the work of another session musician – Sly Dunbar.

You can hear Dunbar's drumming on many of the instrumental LPs. While Sly uses the bass drum to supply a steady, marching beat, he improvises on the cymbals, the snares and the tom toms to produce a multi-layered effect, rather like West African religious drumming.

Again, Rastafarian "ridims" have played an important part in this development. Dunbar has himself been influenced by Rasta drumming patterns. His style is partly modelled on the work of an older session man, Leroy "Horsemouth" Wallace who now plays for the successful reggae group, Inner Circle. Wallace seems to have invented the rockers' rhythm for an early recording made in 1969 for Sir Coxsone Dodd entitled *Things a Come up to Bump*. And Wallace had been part of the original ska generation. He had attended the Alpha reformatory alongside Roland Alphonso and Don Drummond and, as we've seen, it was this group of musicians who led the way for the ska sound by combining Rasta "ridims" with black American music.

But to understand the development of rockers and heavy instrumental dub, we have to go back to the early days of the sound system recordings. We have seen how djs like Duke Reid and Prince Buster used to add spice to the instrumental records they were playing by shouting out their favourite catchphrases over the microphone. These talk overs or toasts soon became a popular feature of the blues dances. After a while, the djs began adding electronic sound effects – echo and reverb – to make the records sound even more unusual. Gradually, as we've seen, more sophisticated recordings were made, using a number of different instrumental and vocal tracks.

One day, King Tubby, a record engineer, was working in his studio mixing a few ska "specials" (i.e., exclusive recordings) for Sir Coxsone's Downbeat system. He began fading out the instrumental track, to make sure that the vocals sounded right. And he was excited by the effect produced when he brought the music back in. So instead of mixing the specials in the usual way, he cut back and forth between the vocal and instrumental tracks and played with the bass and treble knobs until he changed the original tapes into something else entirely. These were the first ever dub records, and they soon helped to draw the crowds to Coxsone's sound. Soon other producers were experimenting with these *dubs*. By the late 1960s, Bunny Lee was putting a dub "version" of the title track on the flip side of all his singles.

On the dub the original tune is still recognisably there but it is broken up. The rhythm might be slowed down slightly, a few snatches of song might be thrown in and then distorted with echo. The drums and bass will come right up to the listener and demand to be heard. Dermott Hussey, a Jamaican record producer, explains what modern dub is like:

> "The dub now is just the bare bones, the rhythm played, bass line of course over-emphasised. And it's just a naked dance rhythm."[1]

Nowadays, Jamaican studios contain equipment which can handle up to twenty-four tracks instead of just two, and the potential for experimentation in dub is vast. Over the past few years, some producers like "Scratch" Perry and Joe Gibbs have experimented with dub to such an extent that the music is beginning to resemble modern, free-form jazz. The original tune is stretched, broken and bent into the most extraordinary shapes by all kinds of electronic wizardry. For instance, on *Africa Dub*, in addition to the usual echo and reverb effects, producer Joe Gibbs has added what sound like car horns, cuckoo clocks, electronic buzzes, bells and pips, and even bomb blasts, to make the record sound unique.

But the early sound system recordings gave rise to yet another type of music within reggae – the dj talk over. As we've seen, Prince Buster's style had been loosely based on the dj "toasts". But it wasn't until 1967 that anyone tried to make recordings in the talk over style. In that year, Lester Sterling produced *Sir Collin's Special* in which he actually *spoke* over the rhythm. King Stitt followed one year later with three dj hits.

Then in 1970, the first big talk over star, U Roy, emerged. U Roy (real name Ewart Beckford) had begun as a dj for King Tubby's system. The weird rambling monologues which he spoke into the microphone over Tubby's sound soon won him a large following. Eventually, he decided to cut some toasting records. He would take a popular rhythm track, phase out the singing and add his own stream of screeches, yelps and muttered catchphrases. The records were an immediate success and U Roy went on to produce a number of classic talk overs with titles like *Wear You to the Ball*, *Flashing My Whip* and *Tom Drunk*. It's hard to find words to describe U Roy's outlandish style. Stephen Davis suggests that it sounds like "a hundred severely ruptured parrots".[2] These early talk overs are certainly wild; at times U Roy sounds almost possessed. U Roy's toasts resemble the inspired ravings of a worshipper "trumping in the spirit" at a Pocomania gathering.

By 1972, other dj artists were challenging U Roy's leadership of the talk over scene. The "King" was soon displaced by younger men. But he made a comeback in 1975 with an LP called *Dread in a Babylon* which sold well both in Britain and Jamaica. As the title suggests, U Roy drew on the Rastafarian imagery of dreadlocks and ganja for this LP. But his style remained basically unchanged. The toasts were just as crazy and full of blistering asides as they had ever been. And for a while the album reinstated U Roy at the top of the toasting league.

In the meantime, other talk over stars had emerged. Dennis Alcapone enjoyed a brief period of success around 1974, when he had hits with records like *Cassius Clay*. But the two major challengers for U Roy's title were I Roy and Big Youth. I Roy (real name Roy Reid) was extremely popular during the mid 1970s. His voice was somewhat deeper and fuller than U Roy's. He would lace his toasts with snatches of song and nursery rhymes. Though his talk overs are frequently comic (listen, for instance, to the early *Welding*), I Roy also presents himself as a wise man "cooling out the youth". For example, I Roy's 1977 album *Crisus Time* was filled with sincere fatherly advice. And on his classic single *Black Man Time* (1974) I Roy solemnly counsels the youth to leave the street corners and to support the literacy programme which the government had just launched. Against a strange, discordant, almost oriental-sounding background of electric violins, I Roy delivers the following sermon:

"I talk to break oppression and set the captives free
So you got to understand I talk to rule the musical
Nation with justice and equality.
So black man you got to be free like a bird in a tree,
And live in love and unity for I and I.
So maybe you can make it if you try.
Say it's a black man time. It a black man time."

Again, you can hear echoes of the old African boast songs in talk over reggae. Just like Trinidad's calypsonians, the djs often strike "bad man" poses. They also tend to mock their rivals with jokey insults and put downs, just as in the 1940s Trinidad's singing stars carried out boasting battles in the *sans humanité* calypsoes. A whole string of I Roy's hits attacked another dj star, Prince Jazzbo, and Jazzbo retaliated by using his own insulting talk overs. In *Straight to Jazzbo's Head*, I Roy taunts his rival with the line: "Jazzbo if you were a jukebox, I wouldn't put a dime into your slot". Jazzbo's counter-attack was rather lame by comparison. In *Straight to I Roy's Head*, he accused his "enemy" of copying U Roy's style: "I Roy, you a boy – move out de way – 'cos you imitate the great U Roy".

But the most popular dj of recent years has undoubtedly been Big Youth. Big Youth (real name Manley Buchanan) is the spokesman for the Rasta influenced youth. His early *skank* records (*Ace 90 Skank*, *George Foreman*, *Foreman and Frazier*, *Screaming Target*, etc.) were basically dance tunes and dealt with the usual rude boy concerns of motor bikes, boxing and "keeping your cool". But his later albums, particularly *House of Dreadlocks*, *Dreadlocks Dread* and *Natty Cultural Dread* made him almost as popular as Bob Marley with the Rastafarian youth. His style is peppered with grassroots patois and secret Rasta phrases:

"When the Lion is sleepin' don't try to wake him, baby...
Then you walk with the idren, down in a Babylon,
You talk with the idren, down in a Babylon,
You can't walk free, down in a Babylon."

Big Youth stresses "dread" and vengeance. His "toasts", in contrast to I Roy's, are filled with threatening prophecies and images of brooding violence which are underlined by the heavy reggae rhythms:

"and di blood goin' flood and di blood goin' run
Blood up town an' blood down town.
An' di blood roun' town.
Blood in di woods and di blood in di country
Marcus Garvey word."

The sinister tone of Big Youth's records calls to mind some of the poems of the Haitian Griot group. Both Griot poetry and Big Youth's dread sounds show a deep awareness of social injustice and racial discrimination. Both teach black pride and fight fire with fire using the idea of Africa to summon up images of darkness and blood.

On *Lightning Flash*, for instance, Big Youth flashes (shakes) his dreadlocks and waits for Judgement Day when, the Bible says, the wicked will suffer and "the righteous black man stand". And the rhythm track in the background fairly pulsates with dread. In fact, it is possible that there is a direct connection with Rasta ridims. One writer has claimed that Big Youth uses his voice to improvise across the reggae rhythms like the repeater in Rasta drumming sessions. The way that he does this derives directly from the Rastafarian Grounation ceremony, in which a singer will lead the other brethren in prayer by toasting over the drums.

Talk over and dub have had a mixed reception from the reggae audience. The music is extremely popular with the young sound system fans. But the Jamaican radio stations have banned it because of pressure from the musicians' union. The union is indignant that the musicians who record the original versions (which then get transformed into dub and talk over records) don't get any royalties. And one tune, one set of ridims, can spark off a host of different versions.

There has always been a relaxed attitude to musical ownership and copyright in Jamaica. In many ways, it was because the island's music scene was so chaotic and disorganised in the early 1960s that reggae could develop from such a wide range of sources. And the Rastafarians had set the tone by "capturing" European hymn tunes and using them for their own purposes. Thus, the Mighty Diamonds feel quite happy about basing their hits on other people's ridims:

"It's not like we stealing anything from anybody. We take a ridim and update it and re-record it. And then we apply our new ideas to it. We call it 'anointing' the ridim with our own magic."[3]

But dub has taken this tendency a lot further. At one time in 1976 there were no fewer than twenty-five different versions of the tune *I'm Still in Love with You* by, among others, Marcia Aitken, Trinity, the Mighty Two, Clint Eastwood, Junior Murvin, the Mighty Diamonds, I Roy, Ranking Trevor, Alton Ellis, Hortense Ellis and Queen Tiney. And many of these artists are talk over djs.

Others accuse talk over of reducing reggae to a set of predictable clichés. Big Youth has spawned a thousand imitators, all claiming to be the true representatives of roots and the Ethiopian connection. And in the last few years there has been a glut of toasting records, many of which are dull. However, Tapper Zukie has won a formidable reputation and more recently Prince Far-I and Prince Hammer have released records. And Dr Alimentado (Winston Thomson) is a true original, with eccentric toasts such as the mysteriously named *She Weng Yep* (also known as "Best Dressed Chicken in Town").

But quite apart from the contributions of individual artists, dub and talk over are important because they are the basic material of the sound systems. And it is the sound systems which are largely responsible for keeping the traditions and the spirit of reggae music alive. It is here at the grassroots level that many of reggae's fads and fashions emerge – new dances, new attitudes, new tastes and trends. In 1976 one London sound system operator talked about the popularity of dub:

"The people dem love fe hear strictly dubwize music 'cause dread dancing is comin' back into fashion. More rocking and swinging kinda movements – and steppers too."[4]

The sound system provides an opportunity for the grassroots people to talk back, to respond, to choose what they like and don't like. At the blues dances, the people can dictate the djs' choice of sounds. And each sound system has its own toasting heroes who can express the feelings of the crowd. I Roy puts it this way:

"We work as the media through which the people speaks, y'know. It's not just us suffering 'cos we're thinking for everybody."[5]

And often the talk over artist, like the calypso singer, can help to clarify local opinion on social and political issues. For instance, Big

Youth, who has been called the "human *Gleaner*" (the *Gleaner* is Jamaica's most popular daily newspaper), produced a record called *Green Bay Killing* about a murder that had occurred on the island a few days before. Within a week, Big Youth's version was matched by Jah Lloyd's *Green Bay Incident* – another dj commentary on the same event. In the same way, Tapper Zukie produced a record called *Ten Against One* about the riots in 1976 at London's Notting Hill Carnival, which was being distributed within days of the disturbances. Often in Jamaica, talk over is a way of getting round the libel and sedition acts. I Roy explains:

> "The music is a way of getting the thing across because . . . you couldn't come out in public and say bluntly maybe somebody would hit you on the head or a copper would take you in for public mischief. [But] you can say it on record and get away with it. Y'know, it's a way of protesting against certain things, against certain physical and mental things that we Jamaican people have suffered."[6]

This process of feed-back – of three-way flow between artists, record producers and the audience – is what helps to make reggae different from other types of pop music. The distance between the performer and the fans is never allowed to grow too great.

And it is at the sound system that the barrier between the fans and the stars is least noticeable. There is always a chance that a record company will discover local talent "toasting a version" over the microphone of a small sound system in a hired hall or club. That is how Glen Sloley, a young talk over artist, began his recording career in England. The old competitive atmosphere of the blues dance still survives in Britain, where sound systems were set up in every ghetto area where West Indians settled. Sloley was a regular at London's Bouncing Ball Club. Every Friday night, Admiral Ken, the resident dj, would play a dub and invite members of the audience to do a version over the microphone. Glen was keen to win and used all his spare time to practise for the next week's competition:

> " . . . is just pure hands vote, y'know. Ken and two other men count the people's hands. The winner would get about £20 and second get nothing, and Bank Holidays it went up to £30 or £35 . . . hard practice a rhythm for the weekend that was truly my work: indoors going over and over the rhythm till I get it perfect. 'Cos I knew that when Friday come if I win there's a money in my hand."[7]

And eventually, after winning eight competitions in a row, Sloley was spotted and signed up by a record company. So dub and talk over help to keep reggae healthy and alive by providing an opportunity for ordinary people to talk back to the industry either as fans with preferences for certain kinds of music, or more directly as talk over djs.

Dub and talk over have had one more effect on the Jamaican record industry which may seem, at first sight, to conflict with the point that's just been made. The stress on recorded ridims in dub has tended to concentrate even more power in the hands of the producers. We have seen how reggae has always been basically recorded rather than live music (though groups like Third World and Bob Marley and the Wailers have opened up the possibility of reggae performance). But both the Jamaican record industry and the music itself grew out of the sound systems. And for the most part, reggae still develops in accordance with the needs of the sound system operators and their fans.

In recent years, because of dub, reggae has become even more studio-based. Each studio has its own recognisable house-style dictated by the producer. For instance, Augustus Pablo at King Tubby's studio produces what he calls the "Far East Sound" featuring an instrument called the melodica. Meanwhile in the mid-1970s, Lee Perry's Black Ark studio released a string of records all with the same identifiable sound – slow, thudding bass lines and heavy ridims. This batch of records included Junior Murvin's *Police and Thieves*, Max Romeo's *War in a Babylon*, the Upsetter's best-selling dub LP *Sugar Ape* and a talk over LP by Jah Lion (Pat Francis) entitled *Columbia Colly*.

But this emphasis on the studio sound doesn't mean that the music has become narrower and more "commercial" as a result – far from it. As we've seen, the situation is still flexible. Musicians move from one session to the next and jam in different combinations and different studio bands. And the producer is not just a manipulating Scrooge, feeding off young talent. For in dub the skill of the record producer and the studio engineer in using the electronic medium is so great, and so crucial, that they have become genuine artists in their own right.

Chapter Eleven

Dread in a Inglan

"A top sound system is thirty to one hundred times as powerful as a domestic hi-fi. The point isn't volume, but the amplification of the bass until it sounds like the world's biggest drum, until it becomes music you can *feel*. You feel it in your feet, in the vibrations of a Coke tin with an unlicensed shot of scotch inside, you feel it through your partner's body. The first time you hear it, it's unbelievable, unbearable, oh my God! But you get used to it. You grow numb, through that and there's a cool, cool joy, a sedative high. Ice in the spine. No pain."

    (Colin McGlashan, "Reggae, Reggae, Reggae, *Sunday Times*, 4/2/73)

That was written by a journalist in England, and he wasn't talking about one of Kingston's sound systems. He was describing a blues dance he'd attended in a black area of London. For the thousands of West Indians who settled in Britain during the boom years of immigration from the 1950s to the mid-1960s brought their music and their culture with them. And within a few years, every major British city with a sizeable West Indian population was beginning to shake to the sounds of ska and reggae.

Like the first "movement of Jah people" from Africa to the West Indies during the days of slavery, the migration of black people to England after the Second World War was a result of Britain's labour needs. Just as in the old days, the sugar barons had imported slaves to work on their plantations in the West Indies, so in the 1950s the British government encouraged the descendants of the slaves – black West Indians – to immigrate to fill the labour shortage. There were simply not enough British workers to do all the jobs that needed doing. And though they had been promised skilled and semi-skilled work, they found, on their arrival, that they were expected to do the menial jobs that English people didn't want. They became cleaners and porters; they worked on the buses and the trains; they were forced to do whatever work was offered.

They tended to settle in the same parts of the same big cities. They were drawn to these areas for a number of reasons. Finding themselves stranded in a strange and often hostile environment, they tended to stick together. Many racially prejudiced landlords refused to house black people, and newly arrived immigrants looking for accommodation were all too often turned away by prospective landlords with the short, sharp phrase: "Sorry, no coloureds". The usual excuse was that coloured neighbours would "lower the tone of the neighbourhood". But the houseowners also feared that black tenants would bring down the price of property in the area.

However, there were other unscrupulous landlords who were quite willing to exploit the immigrants' desperate situation. They crammed as many West Indians as possible into the crumbling tenement houses of the cities' poorer areas. They demanded the highest rents the immigrants could afford – rents which bore no relation to the dilapidated rooms they were offering. Then they allowed the property to deteriorate even further by refusing to keep it properly maintained for their tenants. And so the inevitable happened. White people who had lived in these areas all their lives moved out. And because the landlords had created slums, property prices did indeed fall. The newspapers began to carry sensational stories of black people "living in squalor ten to a room" (as if they had chosen to do so). Areas like London's Paddington, Brixton, Shepherd's Bush and Notting Hill became ghettoes. Faced with discrimination, prejudice and the prospect of poor jobs, poor housing and poor lives, the immigrants began to seek refuge in their own, West Indian culture. And if life was hard and the climate cold and inhospitable, they could always escape to the blues dance:

> "... anywhere you find more than two Jamaicans, any country...on a Saturday night you must have a blues dance. It is something that is in us that when it comes to a Saturday night they get together, they play records, they drink and they dance."[1]

The West Indian way of life survived the transition to Britain. In fact, a truly *Caribbean* culture grew up on British soil because people from all over the British West Indies came to England. And they brought their music with them. At the Notting Hill Carnival, which is based on the "mas" in Trinidad, you can hear reggae, calypso and steel band music. In central London alone there were five clubs which catered in the 1950s for the West Indian crowd: the 59, Flamingo, 77 and Sunset clubs in Soho, and the Contemporanean in Mayfair.

During the 1960s and 1970s Jamaican music always tended to be more popular than the other Caribbean forms with the young West Indian and black British audiences. And Jamaican ska (and later reggae) was easily transported to Britain because, as we've seen, records have always been at least as important as live music in Jamaica. By the early 1960s a few enterprising Jamaicans had set up their own sound systems in Britain's cities, playing imported ska. And the systems were just as competitive as they had been in the West Indies. Singles changed hands at exorbitant prices; deals were made with Jamaican producers and musicians to record exclusive "specials" for the British sound systems.

At the same time, records were imported from the West Indies. Melodisc, set up in 1946 to import jazz and blues records from the USA, began dealing in the 1950s with calypso and Jamaican cover versions of American r&b records. And by the early 1960s Jamaican music was available on the Bluebeat and Planitone (later Orbitone) labels. The first British sound system to rely on Jamaican music was run by Duke Vin in London's Ladbroke Grove. Daddy Peckings, a West London record shop owner, supplied Duke Vin with records on Sir Coxsone Dodd's Studio One label.

By the mid-1960s two other companies – Island Records, and Beat and Commercial (Trojan) – had been set up to promote and distribute the Jamaican sound through shops specialising in black music. It wasn't long before there was a large underground following for ska, particularly among young West Indians and the white youths who lived nearby in the same poor areas. But, with the single exception of Millie's *My Boy Lollipop*, the music had made little impact on the pop charts. It was shunned by the BBC programmers and ridiculed by the radio djs. All too often promotion copies of new singles sent by the record companies to the broadcasting authorities ended up in the dustbin unplayed. The music was considered too raw and crude, the lyrics too obscene and too difficult to follow for white tastes. By the late 1960s, Jamaican music began to be condemned for another reason. For as ska gave way to rocksteady and reggae, Britain had its own version of the rude boy cult.

As in Jamaica, the rude boys were drawn to those sound systems where the heavy roots reggae records were played. By 1968, new sound systems run by younger men were springing up in all the big West Indian centres. At the Ram Jam in Brixton, the crowds "stepped" to Sir Coxsone's sound while to the east in Dalston at the 007, Count Shelley kept the people dancing to his own Jamaican imports. Every Saturday night at civic halls and public baths in Britain's big cities, competitions would be staged between rival sound systems. Each system had its young supporters. They would gather to defend their reputation as the boss side by dancing better, cursing louder and looking cooler than the rest. Britain's rude boy style began to take shape: the trousers and the hair grew shorter, the braces narrowed down until Britain's Johnny Too Bads emerged as a recognisable group.

Then a strange thing happened. At clubs like the A-Train, and the Ska Bar in London where Sir Neville's sound system played, the young white reggae fans began outnumbering the West Indians. To find whites listening to roots music was not in itself unusual. Since the 1950s there had always been some young white people living in the ghettoes alongside the immigrants who were interested in West Indian music. The modernists had been the first sizeable youth group to draw on West Indian style for their inspiration. With the boys in their immaculately pressed Ivy League suits, their Italian shoes, Fred Perry shirts and "stingy brim" hats and the girls in their ski-pants and leather coats, the mods looked as sharp and as dangerous as Al Capone. And though they danced in the main to black American soul, they also did the bluebeat to the early sounds of ska. In 1964, Prince Buster's *Madness*, one of the first ska records to deal with the theme of violence, was a particular favourite with the mods.

But it wasn't until the late 1960s, when the rude boys began to hit the city streets, that the Jamaican music really began to attract a large white audience. By this time, the mod craze had died down. But groups of white youths began attending the sound systems, and especially those based around the town centres. At the Ska Bar in London, the white reggae fans began mixing with the black rudies and copying their style. And out of this contact emerged the white British skinhead – close-cropped hair, Ben Sherman shirt, braces, crombie coat and trousers ending high above the ankle to reveal a great polished pair of Dr Martin boots. The style caused a sensation. The newspapers were filled with outraged headlines about skinhead violence, and soon the craze was sweeping through the nation's poorer city areas.

Some Jamaican artists began making records aimed exclusively at the British skinhead fans. In 1969, Symrapip released a single called *Skinhead Moonstomp*. In the same year, Desmond Dekker's *Israelites* topped the British charts largely because of its popularity amongst the skinheads. But in general, reggae stayed underground. In fact, because it was labelled "skinhead music", reggae became even less acceptable to the BBC programmers than before. "Respectable" music critics went on calling reggae "repetitive" and "moronic". And because production standards in the Jamaican record industry were still not as high as in Europe and the States, most white djs felt justified in dismissing the music out of hand. But there was still a high demand for reggae within the West Indian community itself.

In 1968, Trojan and Island were joined by another company – Pama Records – which was set up by three Jamaican brothers to supply that demand. At the same time, the sound systems were thriving. Soon many of the djs and sound system operators set up their own record shops and distribution networks. Count Shelley, who ran one of the biggest and most popular London systems during the late 1960s, was typical of this new generation of djs. He had arrived in Britain in 1962. By working during the day and presiding over his sound system at night, he gradually acquired the necessary money and know-how to set up his own record business:

> "I was a bricklayer first seven years here. And naturally I check out the sound scene, 'cos back home I used to hang around the systems. I keep quiet: working away a bit, then I start doing my own sound. Laying down bricks day, laying out sounds night. By 1969 I chuck the bricks and make a system full-time."[2]

In 1972, Shelley began importing records produced in Jamaica by Bunny Lee and distributing them through a number of roots reggae shops (shops which cater almost exclusively for the black market). Gradually he expanded the business, opening up Third World Records which combined a shop, a distribution set-up, and Shelley's own record label. But though by the late 1960s he was producing his own records using British reggae musicians, imports still accounted for the bulk of his sales.

As far as the West Indian audience is concerned the most popular reggae (in 1979) is still imported from Jamaica. As in the West Indies, the underground, competitive atmosphere of the sound systems has influenced the whole business of buying and selling reggae records in Britain. Records which have not yet been officially released in the UK (called pre-releases) can be bought at specialist shops for as much as three or four times the recommended list price. Often these records become sound system favourites. And sometimes a tune can become so familiar to the fans that, when it's officially released, no one will buy it because they've heard it so frequently at the blues dances. This is one of the reasons why good reggae records fail to make the charts. Another reason is that the researchers who compile the pop charts draw up their lists on the basis of sales from mainstream record shops – which don't stock roots reggae anyway. So the charts give no indication of how much reggae is sold within the West Indian community itself. To make matters worse, the specialist shops do not always welcome strangers. Philroy Mathias of Venture Records, a small British reggae label, has explained how the different ap-proaches to buying records in the normal high street store and the specialist reggae shop can lead to misunderstanding:

> "Our system of buying records is different, see? A white man usually walks into a shop, he knows what he wants and buys it straight. Because ... he's heard it so much on the radio. And if our kids heard it on the radio they could go in

likewise. We've had one or two white shops who've never taken reggae before. They take our stuff – then when I come back a week later they say they don't want any more. And I ask them why and they say: 'The youth gone on too bad, they come in and say play this, then turn it over and put on another one and... man just can't take it.'"[3]

However, despite all the drawbacks, by the mid-1970s reggae had begun to break through to the larger rock and pop audiences. Groups like the Beatles (in *Ob-la-di-ob-la-da*) and the Rolling Stones (in *Cherry, Oh Baby*) and solo artists like Paul Simon (in *Mother and Child Reunion*) began using a watered-down version of the reggae rhythm for the occasional song. And then in 1974, Eric Clapton's version of *I Shot the Sheriff* went to number one, and many white rock fans were encouraged to go back to the original recording by Bob Marley. At about the same time, Island were beginning to promote the Wailers' records just like any other white rock product, and soon a few reggae albums were appearing in the racks alongside soul and Frank Sinatra.

A sizeable white reggae market developed, and some of these record buyers began tracking down the more "ethnic" roots product. Despite the Rastafarian trappings, roots reggae appealed to many young white people. It was "rebel music". It hadn't become smug and self-indulgent like so much of the rock produced by the rich, successful white stars. Reggae stars in general remained in touch with their roots. They tried to stay close to their fans. Above all, they sang songs about poverty, desperation and revolt – songs which related to the everyday experience of many white kids. So it was that in the late 1970s a new subculture of young whites emerged to champion roots reggae – the punks.

Punk rock and reggae

"We're gonna have a party
It's a punky reggae party.
The Wailers will be there,
The Slits, the Feelgoods and the Clash.
Rejected by society, treated with impunity, protected by
   their dignity."

(Bob Marley)

"I heard a white guy in a college here [in the UK] and I thought it was Sly Dunbar. I was standing outside the hall and I couldn't see who was playing and I said 'Man, who's in there playing? Is that a Jamaican drummer?' And I went in

and there was this guy sitting down with a ring in his ear...
the whole works, punk boots and everything and he was...
cooking. I tell you that. The guy was slapping the rockers. I
couldn't believe it."

(*Cat Coore*, guitarist with Third World)

At first sight the punks seemed unlikely reggae fans. With their dyed
spikey hair, ripped T-shirts and day-glo bondage trousers, they
looked completely different from the black British reggae fans.
What's more, the Rasta creed of "peace and love" didn't seem to fit in
at all with the punk rockers' violent image. But though the frantic,
bug-eyed style of punk rock was totally at odds with reggae's slow,
moody beat, there were obvious similarities between the two types of
music. The punks talked about Britain's crisis in much the same
way as roots reggae artists dwelt on the decline of Babylon. Both
punk and reggae in Britain were rooted in the city and in city
experience. Even the titles of the songs seemed alike: *Anarchy in the
UK*; *War in a Babylon*. And, as Bob Marley suggested in his record
Punky Reggae Party, punks and Rasta youth had something else in
common. Both groups were "rejected by society" and discriminated
against on the grounds of their appearance and beliefs.

Record shops like Rough Trade in London, which catered mainly
for the punks, began selling roots reggae too. And in 1977 the Clash
produced their own punk rock version of Junior Murvin's hit, *Police
and Thieves*. Many young punks had grown up with black British
youths and had gone to the same schools. And when political parties
like the National Front tried whipping up public opinion against the
black communities many punk groups fought back by joining Rock
Against Racism (RAR). Rock Against Racism was set up to combat
racial discrimination in rock music and British society in general.
Soon British reggae groups like the Cimarons and Steel Pulse were
appearing on the same bill as punk bands at RAR concerts. In April,
1977, a march was organised by the Anti-Nazi League through
London's East End where the National Front were gaining ground.
And the march ended at Victoria Park in Hackney, where punk and
reggae groups played to entertain the crowd. But the movement
wasn't all one way. Some reggae artists responded to punk as well.
Bob Marley released *Punky Reggae Party* in 1977, and in 1979 a talk
over artist called Militant Barry produced a record called *Pistol Boy*
dedicated to the recently deceased Sid Vicious.

Once more the record industry was quick to exploit the new
interest in reggae which the punks had helped to stimulate. Virgin, in
the late 1970s still a relatively new but expanding record company
with a chain of shops throughout the country, began signing up
reggae acts. At the same time, a host of independent reggae labels

were formed to plug the gap left by the collapse of the Trojan empire in 1975. These new and sometimes shortlived "indie" labels included names like Grove Music, D-Roy, Klik, Burning Sounds, Venture and Ballistic. And in 1977 Virgin produced their first budget reggae "sampler" (a low-priced album containing tracks from a number of different artists). It was called simply *The Front Line* and included tracks by, amongst others, U Roy, I Roy, the Mighty Diamonds and the Gladiators. The album cover was very dramatic – a black hand covered in blood was shown grasping a single strand of barbed wire – and the LP sold well over 80,000 copies. A marketing executive for the company explained how Virgin was giving roots reggae the "hard sell" treatment.

> "We'll be sending out a lot of promotion material to high street stores, just like we do with the pop artists – posters, streamers, special displays. The same thing goes for radio, we send our pluggers into the BBC and ... the radio stations all around the country. And we also give a lot of records away, not just to the music press but to all the local papers."[4]

Soon other established record companies followed Virgin's example and began signing up and promoting reggae acts.

White artists (even Bob Dylan) went on using reggae rhythms. But by 1979 there had been a new departure. White groups began playing reggae – not just the occasional number but whole reggae repertoires. By this time, the punk craze had died down and the skinhead and mod styles were revived. These latter-day mods and skinheads began to take an interest in the early ska and rocksteady records which had attracted the original subcultures in the 1960s. Eventually groups like the Specials, Selecter and Madness were formed to play ska music live.

The Specials were the first British ska group really to break through nationally. There were seven of them – two black and five white – and they came from Coventry in the West Midlands. They began by playing punk and reggae but found that the two styles didn't mix together musically. So they returned to the Jamaican roots – to ska. The audiences also found ska music better to dance to than either new wave or dub, and the Specials were soon a big success on the club circuit. Dressed in shiny mohair suits and bluebeat hats, they performed spirited versions of tunes like The Pioneers' early reggae classic *Long Shot Kick the Bucket*. Meanwhile at the front of the stage, hordes of teenaged skins and mods would do the shuffle and the shake, while the hall rang to shouts of "Rude Boy" and "Rocksteady". The group's first single, *Gangsters (AKA)*, which was based on the old Prince Buster hit *Al Capone*, sold very well in new wave shops. And the Specials also helped set up a record label – Two Tone – in order to develop a new type of rock music. In an interview, one of the Specials explained that whereas most other types of rock are based on black American blues, soul and r&b, the new form would grow out of Jamaican ska, rocksteady and reggae.

The Selecter were another Coventry-based group who specialised in ska. Their single *On My Radio* successfully blended the ska beat and new wave vocals. The group's line-up was an interesting mixture too. It included a white guitarist, a black bassist sporting dreadlocks and a young woman lead singer. Dressed in a mohair suit, and a pork pie hat, Pauline Black would stomp, glower and shake her fists at the fans – a strutting female rudie. This was a new departure. Though since the early days of bluebeat there had always been a few girl singers in Jamaican music (e.g., Millie Small), women had never played a prominent part in the new sound.

During the late 1960s and early 1970s, as reggae artists and producers became more and more influenced by the Rastafarian doctrine, girls had in fact been positively discouraged from performing. True, some solo female performers had won through against the prejudice and the patronising attitudes of the male-dominated Jamaican music business. Hortense Ellis had won a big following in the 1960s and Marcia Griffiths, later of the I-Threes, the Wailers' backing group, had had a major international hit in 1969 with *Young, Gifted and Black*. The I-Threes – Marcia Griffiths, Judy Mowatt and Rita Marley – are the most famous and the most accomplished of these harmony backing groups. They added a strong, sweet melodic line to the Wailers' music. Dressed in loose African robes and headscarves, they projected an image of powerful dignified Rasta womanhood. After Bob Marley's death, they all recorded solo albums (Marcia Griffiths' *Steppin'*; Judy Mowatt's *Black Woman*; Rita Marley's *Who Feels It Knows It*). In 1979, Sandra Puma Jones, one of a younger generation of black female singers, joined Black Uhuru on the Island label. Jones' songs continued to develop the message of Rastafari for a female audience. *Shine Eye Girl*, for instance, stressed the need for women to look "natural" and stay true to one man, condemning cosmetics and flirtation.

There have been other occasional exceptions to the all-male rule. For instance in 1977 two young Jamaican girls, Althea and Donna, had a number one hit in Britain with a song called *Up Town Top Ranking*. But generally, women have not been encouraged to play an active part in the music. The emergence of a group like The Selecter is therefore a sign of how far things have changed, at least in British reggae. And as reggae moves closer to the mainstream of British society and becomes more generally accepted, it seems likely that young, black British women will begin to find their voice in the music.

Reggae does seem to have at last broken through to a larger audience in Britain. At the time of writing (July, 1979) there are two reggae-influenced records in the British top ten – *Living on the Front Line* and *Babylon Burning*. The first is by Eddy Grant, a West Indian resident in Britain. But the second, despite its title, is new wave rather than reggae, and is by a white group called the Ruts. As a final sign of reggae's growing acceptability, there is now a play called *Reggae Britannica* on the West End stage at the ultra-trendy Royal Court Theatre in London's West End. And the advertisements, aimed at the young, educated middle-class audience, promise "original roots, rockers, reggae live on stage with dub-wize selection!".

But elsewhere in Britain, reggae is still neglected by the British radio networks. And what does get played tends to get lost in the welter of soul, disco, pop, punk and heavy rock. In the 1970s, reggae remained essentially black music – the music of the front line, played by black people for black people.

Black British reggae

> "Handsworth means us the Black People
> Handsworth means us the Black People.
> We're talking now, Speaking Jah Jah people."
>
> *(Steel Pulse,* Handsworth Revolution*)*

Little has changed in the black community in Britain in the last twenty years. Housing still tends to be bad and in the late 1970s, as unemployment soars, even the menial jobs are hard to come by. But the mood amongst some black British youth has changed. They have become more angry and bitter. As relations with the police have got steadily worse over the past few years, the reggae theme of "tribal war in a Babylon" has come to seem more and more relevant. And some black youths don't only listen to reggae now. They have bought their own instruments and begun playing their own brand of British reggae.

This is how British reggae groups like Steel Pulse, the Cimarons, Matumbi, Aswad, Misty and Delroy Washington started. David Hinds of Steel Pulse has explained how reggae compensated for his disappointment at the lack of opportunities facing him on leaving school:

> "As soon as you leave school you find that all the things you were promised – a job, a future and so on – it's all different.

When you realise that, all you've got to turn to is your own culture and yourself. There's nowhere else to look. A black man doesn't get much say in the way things are run outside music. That's why music is so important. The music becomes the message."[5]

Most of the British reggae groups are Rasta-influenced at the moment. And many of the songs reflect the familiar themes of Jamaican reggae – Haile Selassie, Ethiopia, Back to Africa and so on. But at the same time, the lyrics often refer quite directly to the conditions facing black people in Britain. For instance, songs by Aswad like *Three Babylon* and *Can't Walk the Streets* deal with the problems of police harassment and the notorious "sus" law (the Suspected Persons Act, whereby the police can arrest anyone suspected of planning to commit a crime without any evidence). Steel Pulse's first album, *Handsworth Revolution*, was dedicated to the people of Handsworth (Birmingham) where the group lives. Tracks like *Ku Klux Klan* tackled British racism indirectly by referring to the US racist organisation centred in the American deep south. And the group performed the song wearing KKK style white hoods to hammer the point home, should anyone fail to grasp the meaning of the lyrics.

Perhaps the best indication of the quality of this music is that some of it is now becoming popular in Jamaica itself. For example, Matumbi are a successful reggae band who had a hit in Jamaica in 1977 with their single *After Tonight*. Even though they look to Africa for inspiration, they recognise that they now have roots in England too:

"Africa may be the homeland, the mother country of the world, so who shouldn't relate to Africa? But at the moment we're in the UK and that's where our music is coming out strong."[6]

Many of the British reggae groups hold to the Rasta line that all politics are evil and that Babylon will fall without their help if left to its own devices. However, the trend towards British themes in homegrown reggae has led to a more direct approach to questions of race, policing and politics. Recently Cool Ghoul Records released a talk over single by The Phantom called *Lazy Fascist* which attacked political parties like the National Front directly. In an interview, The Phantom explained that he felt the Rastas were playing into the hands of groups like the NF who want to repatriate black people by force:

"[They] love to hear the Rastas talking about repatriation 'cos it makes their jobs a lot easier."[7]

British reggae came of age in the work of the reggae poet, Linton Kwesi Johnson. Linton Johnson was born in Jamaica in 1952 and came to Britain eleven years later. After attending school and college, he was drawn for a time to the Rasta movement. But he soon came to believe that the Rastafarians did not hold the answer for black people in Britain. In his own words, he recognised that "you have to accept that home is where you are at any given time. And you have to make up your mind to confront life as it faces you." He began writing poetry based on his own experiences of life as a young black man in Britain. But he wrote to the rhythm and the beat of reggae music. The poems were often also about reggae – about sound systems and reggae artists – and they were written in Jamaican patois – the language of reggae.

Eventually, in 1977, he recorded an LP for Virgin entitled *Dread, Beat and Blood* in which he read out some of his poems over a heavy reggae backing. The words complement the music perfectly. Johnson's voice follows the beat in a flat but powerful monotone. The poems, which are filled with the reggae imagery of blood and fire, leap to life to the pulse of the thundering bass. In *Five Nights of Bleeding*, Johnson describes how the pressure of life in the slums leads to "war amongst the rebels". The pacing and accent of his voice manages to make even the place names sound like accusations:

> "night number two down at SHEPHERD'S
> right up RAILTON ROAD;
> it was a night named Friday
> when everyone was high on brew
> or drew a pound or two worth of kally.
> sound coming down NEVILLE KING'S music iron;
> the rhythms jus bubbling an back-firing,
> ragin and rising, then suddenly the music cut:
> steel blade drinking blood in darkness.
> it's war amongst the rebels:
> madness . . . madness . . . war."[8]

Johnson draws heavily on the vocal style of Big Youth, and one of his poems, *Bass Culture*, is dedicated to the Jamaican star. The menace, the dread and the blood of Johnson's poems are drawn from Big Youth. But Johnson also makes the style his own and moves the talk over to produce a brand new form – reggae poetry.

Recently, Johnson has won the praise of critics. But he is careful to avoid the trap of stardom:

> "I don't want to become too involved [in the music scene]. I
> don't want to become like Bob Marley. I have no ambitions

of being like some sort of super star. Because if I do I'll get divorced from the realities of life, the realities which give me my inspiration."[9]

For Johnson, the roots have become the realities of life in Britain. He refuses to cut himself off from those realities either by becoming a star or by subscribing to the Rasta creed. But in the process, by drawing on his Jamaican musical roots, he has become the first artist living outside Jamaica to produce a genuinely original form of reggae music. Johnson's reggae poems mix the music of three continents and are the result of 400 years of history. But though the reggae rhythm, the language and the dread are Jamaican, and the beat goes right back to Africa, the words deal emphatically with life here in Britain:

> "Right now
> african, asian, west indian and black british
> stand firm in a inglan
> in dis here time y'know.
> for no matter what they say
> come what may, we are here to stay
> here in a inglan
> in dis here time y'know."[10]

The story of reggae music began with the passage from Africa to the Caribbean in a slave ship. We'll end here in England after yet another journey. We've come a long way from that first image of Kunta Kinte shuffling in his chains on the deck of the ship to the sound of the drums and the concertinas. For Linton Johnson's poems leave no room for doubt. The message is clear and direct and uncompromising. There is no way that the "toubob" could have danced and grinned to *that*.

DUB VERSION: RISE AND FALL OF TWO-TONE

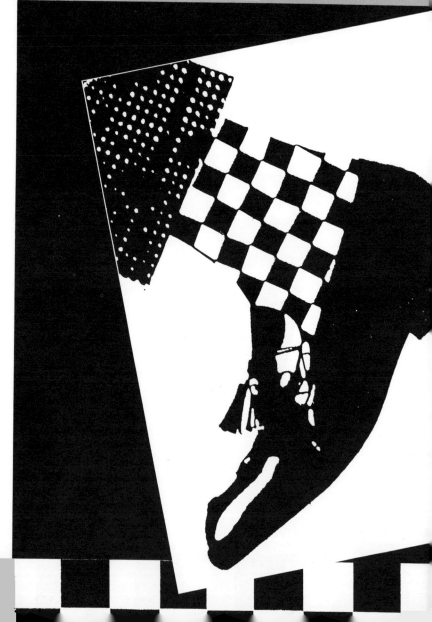

DUB VERSION

Dub version (1982)
(the rise and fall of Two Tone)

Chapter Twelve

Ska Tissue

"All Indians must dance, everywhere, keep on dancing. Pretty soon in next spring, Great Spirit come... All dead Indians come back and live again. They all be strong just like young men, be young again..."

(Wavoka, leader of the Sioux Ghost Dance religion
of the 1880s)

One cold night in Birmingham in 1978, I met Jerry Dammers, keyboard player with Special AKA, then the Coventry Automatics, later still the Specials, at the flat of the group's third manager, Mike "Shoop" Horseman. Crouching on the floor over his sketch pad, Dammers, the man who master-minded Two Tone, looked up from a doodle he'd just completed of a pair of shoes next to the photo of Peter Tosh in his early Wailing Wailers days; the photo which, in negative, was going to be the Two Tone trademark. Dammers looked up and said:

"What I need now is *loafers*. A pair of loafers just to top it off."

Loafers... black slip-ons with a leather tassle across the front, cut low under the ankle with a thick, heavy sole. These talismanic black objects, summoned up like dead relations at a seance, were lumbering back from the past and into the late 1970s where they would stand for Jerry Dammers, as another sign of Two Tone, and later still, as the logo for the Two Tone film. These were the shoes the skinheads used to wear back in 1969 on ska nights down at the city-centre clubs with their tonic mohair suits – the "two tone" suits which changed colour depending on how the light caught them. Now these things were to be worn again, brought back to life along with the cheap, choppy music, the "nutty" dance moves, the sta-prest trousers, the white socks, the Fred Perry sports shirts, the pork-pie hats (a.k.a. "stingy brims" or "blue-beats"). The shoes were just one brick in the edifice, a telling symbol in the Dammers Two Tone Dream.

Dammers knew that if he got the details right – the things that the pernickety young punters noticed – he might be able to swing the whole package. And the package, in this case, consisted not only of an image and a sound but also of an attitude, a posture, amongst other things, on race.

When looking at Two Tone, the point to remember is not that it was, as some rock and reggae purists have suggested, a "media-created hype" (less "authentic" than the original 1960s ska movement), nor that the music produced by the groups (the Specials, the Selecter, Madness, the [English] Beat, the Body Snatchers, UB40, and the Swinging Cats), which gathered beneath the Two Tone banner during its brief and highly-publicised career ripped off the originals, the neglected makers of the black Jamaican musical tradition: Don Drummond and the Skatalites, Prince Buster, Laurel Aitken and the rest. After all, the Two Tone groups hardly concealed their dependence on the first ska phase. Even the names of the bands carried their histories on their sleeves. The Specials took their name from the "special" one-off recordings made for the early sound systems in the days of Duke Reid; and Madness lifted their title from the Prince Buster hit which did the rounds of the British mod dance halls in 1965.

Instead what's important about Two Tone is that Jerry Dammers realised that when dealing with the popular music industry, the important issues for the artist have less to do with staying "honest" and "authentic" and refusing to "sell out" than with grabbing and retaining control of the product at every stage and in all its forms. What he saw was that artists should be concerned not just with writing songs and getting them performed and recorded, but with keeping maximum control over every aspect of production: over record mixes, release dates, label and cover design, promotion, marketing, retail distribution and . . . image. If you could get that kind of control, then you might be able to say something worth saying in the accent and the manner of your choice. But what neither he nor anybody else in 1978 could have predicted was the speed and the scale on which the Two Tone Dream was to take off . . .

Rough trade, smooth deal

Within a year, the Specials had borrowed £700 from a local entrepreneur and used it to record a tribute to Prince Buster's *Al*

Capone called *Gangster*. Rough Trade, the London-based independent label with its roots firmly in "alternative" punk, agreed to handle distribution. The B-side was an instrumental track called *The Selecter*, recorded by Neol Davies and John Bradbury, the drummer with the Specials. Rough Trade pressed 5,000 copies, which were then encased in a snazzy, black-and-white check sleeve designed by Dammers himself. (The b/w check introduced two major themes which were to dominate early Two Tone output: 1960s revivalism (Op Art?) and – more obscurely – the multiracial ideal: black and white adjacent yet separate, different but connected like the squares on a chessboard.)

The record achieved cult status in England within days of its release. It was well received by the music press and by dj John Peel, the BBC's own alternative taste-maker. Soon, Elvis Costello and Ian Dury were showing conspicuous interest. The Specials, *Gangster* and Two Tone were so immediately successful that the group was able to negotiate an unprecedented deal with Chrysalis. The Specials and the newly formed Selecter were made directors of Two Tone, issued with a relatively substantial budget, and given a guarantee by Chrysalis that they would release a minimum of six singles a year, singles chosen exclusively by Two Tone directors. This was a virtual coup, and it opened the way for The Beat to secure a similar deal with Arista in late 1979, setting up their own label, Go Feet.[1]

This shift in the relationship between young recording artists and their record companies had been precipitated largely by the crisis in confidence which permeated the industry in the wake of punk. (How the hell do you tell good music from bad after the Sex Pistols?) But in Britain it opened up the way for more flexible, less cautious signing and management policies. It allowed for more speedy turnover of product and more fluent contact with the young, fickle audience. Incidentally, it accelerated the process whereby new "street" styles and sounds get generated, removing the obstacles and checks which would normally slow down the industry's response to demand. The responsibility for making profits had begun to devolve onto the narrow shoulders of the artists themselves.

Within a matter of months, Dammers and the Specials had stormed the citadel. By the end of 1979, Two Tone music was beginning to figure heavily in the British charts. One edition of BBC Television's *Top of the Pops* featured no less than three new Two Tone singles: the Specials' *A Message To You Rudy*, *One Step Beyond* by Madness and the Selecter's *On My Radio*. The ideals and objectives formed in the frustrating years of provincial anonymity were now, on the face of it, realisable. Dammers' vision of the future was about to have its day.

A documentary vision

The Dammers Dream had been shot in black and white. It had originally consisted of a fusion of rock and reggae. When, in 1977, Horace Panter (Sir Horace Gentleman), Lynval Golding and Jerry Dammers together formed the Coventry Automatics, they sought to reflect the multiracial composition of the group and its music by combining punk and heavy reggae. But as Jerry puts it, when they played the local clubs "the two tended to stay separate. Audiences used to be dancing, then they'd pogo, then they'd give up."[2] They were forced to turn back to ska and bluebeat, back to a less separatist form of Jamaican music than "ethnic" roots reggae.

Other local groups were moving in a similar direction. Neol Davies, founder of the Selecter, began playing bass with a soul-reggae outfit called Chapter 5 in the mid-1970s, whilst Dave Wakely, guitarist with The Beat, set out some years later, in his own words,[3] to mix punk's "high energy" with the "fluid movement" of dub. And Ranking Roger, the group's black front-man and toaster, crossed all the categories: he began (with orange hair) as the drummer in a Birmingham-based punk band called the Dum Dum Boys and toasted with the multiracial reggae band UB40 before opting for the more eclectic sound of The Beat, which draws on rhythms rooted in jazz, West African and Afro-Cuban forms as well as in rock, ska and reggae. The Specials, then, were not the only local group to synthesise black and white expression, black and white experience ... but they were the first to make a really convincing *popular* mix. They were the first to keep the crowd on its feet and dancing throughout an entire set.

Knees Up Mother Brown with coconuts

Behind the fusion of rock and reggae lay the hope that the humour, wit and style of working-class kids from Britain's black and white communities could find a common voice in Two Tone; that a new, hybrid cultural identity could emerge along with the new music. This larger message was usually left implicit. There was nothing solemn or evangelical about Two Tone. It offered an alternative to the well-intentioned polemics of some of the more highly educated punk groups, who tended to top the bill at many of the early Rock Against Racism gigs.[4]

Dammers and the rest had sensed that there was a growing reaction on the part of the working-class rock audience against "message music", a movement away from sixth-form Brecht and crudely anti-establishment lyrics. The Two Tone bands were more interested in harmonising the form and the lyrics, the sound and the sense, so that, without being obtrusive, the multiracial message could be *inferred* by a broadly sympathetic audience.[5] They were giving shape to a sensibility rather than a political programme. Instead of imposing an alien, moralising discourse on a popular form (alien at least to their working-class constituency), bands like the Specials worked in and on the popular, steered clear of the new avant gardes, and stayed firmly within the "classical" definitions of 1950s and early 1960s rock and pop: that this was music for Saturday nights, something to dance to, to *use*.

The politics were there but they were sublimated, as in reggae, to the rhythms. And the rhythms were what pulled the crowds in. Fast and jumpy, they provided the perfect complement for that nervous, wiry kind of dancing idealised by every English inner-city subculture from the original teds of the 1950s through the mods, rudies and skinheads of the 1960s to the Northern Soul fans ten years later. The ideal inner-city dance is a very English affair. Manic yet restrained, it bears little relation to the free-form stuff favoured on the college circuit in the States. (Dave "Shuffle" Steele, guitarist with The Beat, was unimpressed by the dancing he saw during the group's first US tour: "They were all so floppy and out of time," he said. "Actually, they're easily the worst dancers we've found yet."[6]) The inner-city stomp, on the other hand, is improvisation within a tight structure. It's graceful but the grace is always "under pressure". Fred Astaire on leapers.[7] And just as, in the 1930s, Astaire's syncopated tap routines had drawn heavily on negro jazz dancing traditions, so the modern English stomp has its roots in the black West Indies, in the backyard Kingston blues parties. Two Tone made these roots visible. As the sun sets on the British Commonwealth, Two Tone braided musical strands from England, America and the old Caribbean colonies, and turned the wake into a carnival. They gave us the Ghost Dance of the British Empire, played out at the moving point where the pre-war Lambeth Walk meets Peter Tosh's Steppin' Razor: culture-clash converted into fun – *Knees Up Mother Brown* with coconuts.

This didn't stop the bands from making serious statements, but the Two Tone strategy differed fundamentally from punk's. The Specials, the Selecter and the rest had gone beyond the arch, self-conscious nihilism of the Sex Pistols and the angry rhetoric of the Clash. The political objectives of Two Tone were more modest. The targets were more clearly defined: unemployment, the police, and authoritarian government. This shift in strategy was a consequence of larger social and economic pressures. Britain itself had moved, since 1977, into the worst recession since the war. Punk's gloomiest prophecies were realised by a Conservative government pledged to a monetarist policy of massive spending cuts and the systematic demanning of British industry. By 1980, for thousands of British school leavers, there really was "no future": no work, no likelihood of finding work, minimal welfare, and the heightened possibility of nuclear war in Europe. In purely political terms, *No Future*[8], the Sex Pistols' sonic assassination of the Queen, monarchism and "good musicanship", was beginning to sound transparently contrived, almost quaint, almost literary when laid alongside The Beat's straightforward plea to the current Prime Minister, Mrs Thatcher, to "for God's sake, stand down, Margaret".[9]

Concrete jungle

Two Tone grew out of punk, and there were links between the two movements. Punk and Two Tone both cultivated the romance of the street (an important mythical site in the geography of rock, at least since *West Side Story*). The lyrics and the looks of both punk and Two Tone referred more or less directly to what Peter York has called the "1958 council estate teenage greaseball" cluster.[10] They both sought to break the Atlantic connection; both were moved by a desire to tap British experience and to shake off the traditional dependency of British rock on American styles and motifs.

Two Tone music was ska at 78rpm, sung with a nasal English accent, and many of the groups spiced things up with a distinctively British sense of humour which derived from the old music halls and which blended in neatly with the ska tradition of boasting, self-mockery and bad-mouthing developed in Jamaica by men like Buster and Duke Reid. Madness, in particular, play it for the laughs. Their line-up includes an Irish-cockney giant called Chas Smash who, in dark glasses, with a stingy brim tilted to his eyebrows, performs odd, robotic dances. The top half of his body is as stiff as a board, all the movement taking place below the knees. Madness on occasion wear Turkish fezzes (an obscure and rather ancient British joke associated (in 1982) with the stand-up comedian Tommy Cooper, but which goes back at least to the pre-War period).

It's hardly surprising, then, that the Two Tone groups refused to pronounce the "correct", "responsible" line on race. Instead they built on what was already there, and, in the West Midlands at least, there was plenty. The Coventry and Birmingham music scene is in some ways unique in Britain. The rock and reggae communities have never been as segregated there as in London. In pubs in the predominantly black areas of Birmingham's Balsall Heath and

Handsworth, it's not unusual to see black and white musicians of all ages jamming together. Birmingham must be one of the only places left in Britain where it's still possible for a white man to get into a shebeen without wearing a blue uniform and kicking the door down.

So, because a casual basis for exchange existed in the area, the rhetoric of anti-racism could generally be dropped. At the simplest level, the Two Tone bands visibly and audibly demonstrated that racial harmony was a possibility in Britain, at least among disaffected youth. Ranking Roger explained his position on anti-racism in 1981:

> "We don't have to say to people, he's black and I'm white, or I'm black and he's white. We don't say that between songs. I mean, people can see for themselves. If they can't they must be blind or something, because black and white are there. They're playing together and loving every minute of it... that's just love and unity."[11]

However, in this respect some Two Tone fans were both blind and mad. Even at the earliest ska revival gigs, there were fascist contingents amongst the fans: young white supporters of the far-right National Front and British Movement parties. Throughout 1979 and 1980, there were reports in the music press of skinheads chanting *"Sieg Heil"* at Madness concerts. (Madness, the only London ska group, are also the only all-white Two Tone group. They are signed, in fact, to Stiff Records.) Some far-right rudies referred to the Specials as the Specials Plus Two (a symbolic excision of Neville Staples and Lynval Golding, the two original black Specials, subsequently joined on tour by the veteran ska trombonist, Rico Rodriguez).

As things got worse in Britain, and worse still for the black community, who are subject not only to a higher unemployment rate but to vicious, unprovoked attacks from racists, many Two Tone groups began to adopt a more open, less hipsterish stand on the issue. In June, 1981, the Specials organised a Peaceful Protest Against Racism at Butts Athletic Stadium in the Earlsdon district of Coventry in response to an earlier violent protest against the local Asian community – the fatal stabbing in April in the city centre in broad daylight of a twenty-year-old boy called Satnam Singh Gill.

By 1981, the Dream, buckling under "too much pressure", was in danger of falling to pieces. The original Two Tone roster had split up months before. And the idealism of the early days, when the final mix for The Beat's first (and only) Two Tone single *Tears of a Clown* had been decided by a ballot amongst all the Two Tone groups, had become dissipated as the commercial and administrative problems of running the expanding empire began to assert themselves. The

Dream went down under the combined weight of intensive tabloid interest, continuous exposure in the music press and a flood of cheap and nasty spin-offs churned out by outsiders. Two Tone badges, scarves and ties: Specials T-shirts, Selecter socks and Madness tupperware. (The concessions had proved more slippery than Dammers had imagined.) Eventually, he had to face up to the fact that Two Tone had grown beyond his good intentions.

Every Two Tone move was monitored, analysed, assessed as a possible trend. "It's become a monster," Dammers confided to one reporter. "Frankenstein's monster." Finally, he cracked, suffering a breakdown at the mixing desk as he helped produce the soundtrack for *Dance Crazy*, the film of the movement he'd created.

> "I dunno how to describe it," he said later, "but I just went to pieces. I haven't had a week off in the past two years. I've been living out of a suitcase like some sort of tramp...."[12]

The Selecter finally broke away at the end of 1980, and by then the music had long outgrown its origins in ska. By the time the second album, *More Specials*, was released in June, 1980, Dammers had moved from *Long Shot Kick the Bucket* into muzak. Former certainties had already been eroded and discarded along with the self-conscious populism of the early Two Tone output. This had all been displaced by that impatience with the settled and the given, that restless urge to violate existing musical categories and audience expectations which has marked most forms of British rock and reggae at least since punk and 1976.

In the autumn of 1981 at a concert in Cambridge towards the end of the last British tour the Specials were to give, Dammers and Terry Hall, the lead singer, were arrested for "behaviour likely to cause a breach of the peace" when they tried to prevent the crowd from fighting and throwing cans at each other and the stage. They were later found guilty of "inciting violence" and fined £1,000. ("This isn't a town, it's a trained-dog act," muttered Dammers to reporters.) Rumours of a split began to circulate and in late November they were confirmed. Terry Hall, Neville Staples and Lynval Golding had left to form the Fun Boy Three and were about to release a record entitled *The Lunatics (Have Taken Over the Asylum)*. Dammers was reported to be thinking about reforming Special AKA and returning to the original project of opening a studio in Coventry to serve as a launching-pad for local talent. And meanwhile, The Beat were making records about the Bomb.

Ska has been laid to rest again. Meanwhile a new generation of nostalgics is being born – a generation hooked on early Two Tone tapes – who will look back fondly to the time when Two Tone ruled the airwaves and, more especially, to the moment in July, 1981, when it all seemed to crystallise, the moment when, with Britain facing its greatest social and economic crisis since the 1930s, black and white youths clashed with the police in the decaying inner rings of the country's larger cities. As the riots flared in Toxteth, Manchester, Liverpool and London, in Birmingham and Coventry and Wolverhampton, the BBC played the week's National Anthem, the people's choice, the British number one, the Specials doing *Ghost Town*.

> "This town is coming like a ghost town
> Why must the youth fight amongst themselves?
> Government leaving youth on the shelf.
> This town is coming like a ghost town.
> No job to be found in this country."
>
> *(The Specials,* Ghost Town*)*

. . . .

Postscript

> "We're gonna have a party
> It's a punky reggae party.
> The Wailers will be there.
> The Slits, the Feelgoods and the Clash.
> Rejected by society; treated with impunity; protected
>   by their dignity.
>
> (*Bob Marley*, "Punky Reggae Party", 1976)

On the night of 7 January, 1982, at a club in Coventry called Shades, former Special Lynval Golding was attacked without provocation by a gang of white youths and subjected to an assault of such ferocity that the wounds to his face and throat alone were to require twenty-eight stitches. Hospital sources reveal that his eyesight may be permanently impaired. The next day Golding released a statement urging his fans not to retaliate:

> "My music is about peace, and I'm sure the guys who did this to me will feel sorry for what they did, because I'm a guy who wants to live in peace with people . . . It's funny, you know, because I've never thrown a blow at anyone."

The party's over, Marley's punky reggae party. And Marley's dead. We've come a long way in our loafers since the lights went out.

CLUB MIX:
BREAKING FOR THE BORDER

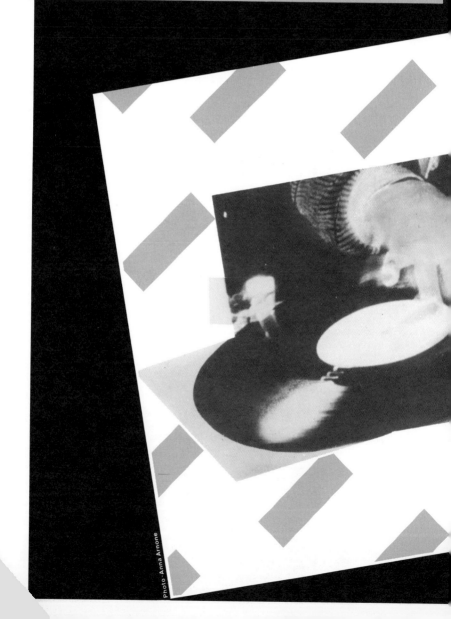

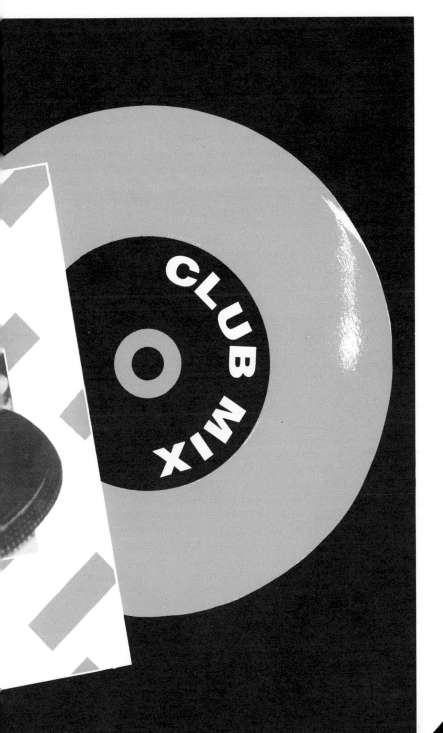

Club Mix (1986)
(Breaking for the border)

Chapter Thirteen

Sister Posse forward: is this the future?

"We have fe kill kill de Police Bill
We have fe kill, kill de Police Bill
Dem in a Panda car dem in a Transit van
Wid dem riot shield and a big truncheon
Dem use plastic bullet and water cannon
Dem fire CS gas pon de mainland
True dem no want a repetition
Of de rebellion in a Brixton
Which tek place in a 81.

Dem sey you carry offensive weapon
Stop and search you pon suspicion
Next ting dem carry you down a station
Ninety-six hours in a detention
And there subjected to interrogation
And also to humiliation.

Dem mek up evidence fe a conviction
To get release have fe mek confession
Same ting dem a do now in Northern Ireland
And now dem a bring it here in England
Dem have de power to set up roadblock
So you better watch out if you poor or you black
You drive you car you bound fe get stop
Remember how Stephen Waldorf get shot.

We have fe kill kill de Police Bill
We have fe kill kill de Police Bill.

'Cause if dis Police Bill become law
Pon de street we a got have pure war

Arm these police like in America
Then you a go see pure massacre.

That's why –
We have fe kill kill de Police Bill."

On the face of it it might seem that little has changed on the reggae scene in the years since I wrote the earlier chapters of this book. These lyrics are from a song released in 1984 called *Kill the Police Bill* and they deal with the classic reggae theme of police harassment. They carry on the protest against unjust laws aimed at the poor and powerless. Reggae can still be a rebel sound. And the music is still being used to build a sense of common interests among black people both here in Britain and abroad. It still acts as a kind of newspaper offering information and comment on current affairs. *Kill the Police Bill* is about the threat to civil rights posed by the Police Bill, which greatly extends police powers of arrest and detention. The record tells us all this. At the same time it reminds us of the Brixton riot in 1981. We remember that the riot was triggered off by Operation Swamp, when police mounted a massive stop and search campaign in the Brixton area. It also reminds us that one year later police shot and almost killed an innocent member of the public, Stephen Waldorf, when they mistook him for a wanted criminal.

And yet the release of this record in the 1980s also proves that many things have changed. First it was made in Britain not Jamaica, and it deals with a *local* political issue. In 1986, black British music is stronger and more confident than it's ever been. In fact, some people would argue that British reggae is now more alive, more interesting to listen to and more in touch with the fans than the music which is coming from Jamaica. Second, the song was recorded by a young woman dj called Ranking Ann (Ann Swinton). Toasting and dj reggae had always been a male preserve in the 1970s but talk over artists like Ranking Ann have shown that women can speak out on a rhythm against social injustice as well as any man. Ann is the first British female reggae MC. (MC originally stood for Master or Mistress of Ceremonies; now it refers to "Mike Chanter".) She began performing at the microphone in her home town of Wolverhampton in 1978. Since then she has released three albums and a string of singles. In the 1980s she has been joined by young MCs like Lorna Gee (Lorna Gayle), Lady Sheree, Pepi, Cindarella and Olive Ranking. In Jamaica, too, women like Queen Tiney, Sister Nancy, Lady Ann, Super Chick and Sister Verna have begun to "chat 'pon a sound" in dj style. Meanwhile, in Britain, Culcha Posse is the first sound system to be operated by a woman, Sista Culcha.[1]

Reggae is at last opening up to new voices and new experiences.

Ranking Ann has turned away from love songs just as many Rasta-inspired male artists did in the 1970s. But she hasn't become a Rasta either. She turns Big Youth's old slogan ("No more songs about girls!") on its head: no more songs about boys! The lyrics here and in songs like *Right to Fight* and *A Wa Do Men* ("you can't find a good one/out of the whole of them!") make it clear that black girls face their own special kinds of pressure. Later in *Kill The Police Bill*, Ann recounts the story of how she was arrested for suspicion on her way home from work and taken to a police station for questioning:

"Thirty-six hours in a detention
And dem wouldn't even let me contact no one
Dem try fe mek a search inside me private region
Sey me conceal a dangerous weapon
And lord me analyse the situation
Mek no mistake it's like legal rape.

And when dem let me out guess what dem tell me
Dem intend to pick me up continually
And hold me in custody
And dem don't even have fe charge me
Lord dem a tek weh we liberty
Wid dem legality."

The third way in which this record differs from a 1960s or 1970s toast is to do with how it was produced. *Kill the Police Bill* was financed by the Greater London Council instead of the usual privately-financed record company. The label carries the words: "Produced by GLC POLICE SUPPORT UNIT". In the first half of the 1980s some of the metropolitan councils in the big British cities defied Westminster by spending more money on social services like public housing and transport than Mrs Thatcher's government wanted them to spend. And some authorities like the GLC also funded minority groups, multi-racial arts programmes, festivals and workshops. This was all stopped in March, 1986, when the Local Government Bill became law and the GLC and the six "offending" metropolitan councils were abolished without people being allowed to vote whether they wanted this to happen or not. But for a brief time in the 1980s reggae and other forms of black British and Caribbean music had got some recognition and support from one of the largest and most powerful city administrations in Europe.

None of this guaranteed the record commercial success. Although it is, in my opinion, a classic reggae cut (both Ann's version and the dub), it failed to make an impact on the charts. It may be that other factors in the music industry have kept reggae out of the charts in recent years. Record sales worldwide have been declining since the late 1970s. And the shift into video promotions has also worked against "minority" musics like reggae. Videos are very expensive to make and they are a risky investment. Few reggae record labels have the kind of money needed to make the sort of video you see on television pop programmes. And this has helped to marginalise the music even further. Reggae rhythms were absorbed into the pop repertoire of internationally successful bands like The Police in the late 1970s and early 1980s. And as the tide of interest has receded, the original reggae musicians and singers have for the most part been left stranded again in a black musical ghetto. But the treatment Ranking Ann's record got from the industry looks a bit more pointed than that. It's not just a case of another reggae record being ignored by the BBC and the local commercial radio stations. What Ranking Ann was saying was just too controversial to get proper hearing.

And it wasn't only radio programmers who refused to play the record. Many roots reggae fans in 1984 didn't like the idea of a girl stepping out of the stereotyped passive female role and "chanting down Babylon" either. On its own, the record wasn't enough to change the course of events. The slogan "keep the GLC working for London" printed on the record sleeve didn't stop the GLC from being abolished. The record didn't manage to kill the Police Bill: the Bill became law in 1985–6. In fact, police powers are now likely to be extended still further. In 1985, the shooting by police in Brixton of another innocent member of the public, Mrs Cherry Groce, led to a second Brixton riot. And one month later, the Broadwater Farm Estate in Tottenham exploded in a violent reaction which ended in the death of PC Keith Blakelock after Mrs Cynthia Jarrett collapsed and died during a search without warrant of her home. In the wake of these incidents the Metropolitan Police chief, Sir Kenneth Newman, has been calling for a further extension of police powers. He wants plastic bullets and tear gas to be made available to British police if and when he thinks they're needed. It seems that Ranking Ann's predictions have been proved true. But despite the fact that *Kill the Police Bill* didn't get played on the radio and didn't manage to kill the Bill, the record *still* stands as a landmark in the history of reggae music. It marks the forward march of the Sister Posse. It shows how different voices are using reggae music in different ways and in different contexts in the mid to late 1980s. But before we look at some of these new developments we have to unravel the mystery of what happened to *Jamaican* reggae in the intervening years.

Chapter Fourteen

Slack style and Seaga

Some people claim that when Bob Marley died in 1981, reggae died with him. They argue that without Marley's charismatic leadership and creative genius, reggae has lost its way and much of its international appeal. Whether or not Marley's death really *did* have a decisive impact on the music as a whole, it is true that nowadays reggae doesn't always seem to grip the imagination of British youth as it once did. This is certainly the case with the music coming from Jamaica at the moment (1986). To understand the decline of Jamaican reggae and the Jamaican record industry we have to look at the wider social and political background.[1]

The decade had opened with the rise to power of Edward Seaga's Jamaican Labour Party (JLP) in October, 1980, after the bloodiest election campaign in the island's history. Over 700 people had been killed in the run up to the election by rival gangs supporting JLP and PNP (People's National Party) politicians. PNP Prime Minister Michael Manley had put the island "under heavy manners" and had introduced tough emergency measures in a vain attempt to control the violence. But the JLP had the support of American business and the White House. Some people claimed that it was also being backed by the CIA. As gun battles raged in the streets of West Kingston and a PNP cabinet minister was murdered in his car, it looked as if Manley's administration was unable to govern.

During Manley's second term of office from 1976 onwards, Jamaica had been plagued by shortages. Even basic things like food and soap were difficult to buy. Since 1972, when Manley first came to power, there had been a steady stream of businessmen flying off the island to Miami. They were unwilling to pay the increased customs duties and taxes to support Manley's socialist policies. Schools and literacy campaigns, hospitals and welfare services, all cost money and it had to come from somewhere. The big loan-giving organisations like the IMF (International Monetary Fund) and the American government were not prepared to finance a socialist administration in the Caribbean. Jamaica was too close to the US shoreline for the Americans to allow this to happen. So the pressure began to fall on local businesses and the multinational companies who ran the major industries on the island (tourism and bauxite). They were asked to provide some of the necessary cash for Manley's socialist programmes. Currency restrictions were imposed, but as the business-men flew off to the States, they took their money with them. Meanwhile, Manley had developed a close working relationship with the neighbouring communist state of Cuba, only ninety miles from the island's northern tip. Cuban advisers were called in to help put Manley's policies into action and teams of Cuban workers were soon building schools in Jamaica.

After Manley was voted back in 1976, the stream of money moving to Miami turned into a flood. It was not only the businessmen who feared a communist take over. The USA had already proved that it was prepared to intervene in the affairs of neighbouring countries if it didn't approve of the government in power. In 1973, the CIA had helped to overthrow the democratically elected Allende regime in Chile. Ten years later President Reagan was to go one step further when he ordered the invasion (on 13 October, 1983) of the Caribbean island of Grenada, run at the time by a Marxist government under the late Maurice Bishop. And throughout the 1980s the Reagan administration has been financing and training the right-wing "contra" terrorists who are using violence in an attempt to bring down the democratically elected Sandinista Government in Nicaragua.

So when Seaga swept to power in 1980 he stood for everything that Manley had stood against. He set out to turn the Caribbean tide away from what Manley had offered. Instead of working towards an economy based on collective ideals, with farms and businesses run as co-operatives, he set out to bring back a free market economy based on competition. He wanted to make Jamaica the Hong Kong of the West. Seaga's opponents claim that in order to achieve this ambition he has made Jamaica little more than an American satellite. It's certainly true that he has close links with the Reagan administration. Seaga was the first foreign head of state to meet with Reagan after he became US President in 1981. And in November of that year, Seaga broke off diplomatic relations with Castro's Cuba. Since then, the money has flooded back to the island. The IMF lent Jamaica $698 million. By 1982, the American Senate had granted a further $100 million in foreign aid. And a syndicate of American businessmen headed by David Rockefeller had offered over $1 billion worth of investments to help make Seaga's dream possible.

All this has had an impact on the island's culture and its sense of national identity. Ultimately it has had an impact on its music too. As we have seen, Michael Manley had lent his support to Rasta-influenced reggae. He had invited Selassie to the island for a state visit in 1966. In election campaigns, Manley had used the language of the Bible to win people's votes. He had stressed the links between the socialist tradition and the Rastafarian search for justice and a spiritual home. After all, wasn't socialism rooted in the same quest for justice and equality that had inspired the Rastafarians? Weren't socialists just as interested as the Rastas in finding a better place to live? The only difference was that Manley said that that better place was here in the Caribbean not back in Africa. Manley set out to make the have-nots feel at home in Jamaica. This was *their* island. *This* could be their Africa. And the links between socialist and Rastafarian beliefs could be made most clearly through reggae music. There were two reasons for this. First, reggae was the perfect medium for expressing all these ideals, hopes and dreams. And, secondly, the record industry could create wealth for the island so that those ideals, hopes and dreams could be put into action.

Seaga was no stranger to the music either. He had been involved in the Jamaican music business from the very early days. As a young man he had recorded Kumina and Pocomania Church music in the Jamaican countryside. Later, as we have seen, he had promoted Byron Lee as a Jamaican pop star and had himself become president of West Indian Records. But when he came to power, Seaga had no stake in the Rastafarian connection which Manley had helped to foster. The Rasta themes of black pride and a place in the sun for the "have-nots" and the "sufferers" did not fit into his idea of what Jamaica and the Jamaican national image should be. For Seaga, Jamaica must be a modern nation able to compete in the capitalist world, not a country of "sufferers" obsessed with their "roots". When Seaga refers to the Manley era as the "dark times" he is referring not just to the violence and chaos of the last few months of the PNP regime. For by linking up with roots and Rasta reggae, Manley was also linking Jamaica's future with the Third World rather than with white America.

When Seaga came to power he set out to break those links once and for all. As the new decade opened, a new mood began to dominate the music. And that mood is most clearly summed up in the rise of *slack style* reggae. Slack style is the name given to the "dirty" talk overs of the new generation of djs headed in the early 1980s by Winston Yellowman Foster. Yellowman's first hits, *Soldier Take Over* and *Operation Eradication*, had criticised the way the Seaga government was using military goon squads to police the ghettoes. But after these early efforts Yellowman stopped dealing with controversial political issues. Instead he began to develop his famous pornographic *slack* toasts. These toasts concentrated largely on insults to women, and on the themes of sex and money and the relationship between them.

As his name suggests, Yellowman is an albino, and he cuts an outrageous figure when he performs. Dressed in camouflage army fatigues or in a bright yellow suit with gold baubles woven into his fair hair, his light eyes hidden behind a pair of square framed tinted glasses, Yellowman would strut onto the stage to the marching strains of "Left! Right! Left! Right!" from the opening bars of *Soldier Take Over*. This became Yellowman's signature tune. The older djs had often taken clownish, "trickster" or "bad man" images. However, despite the bizarre poses of some of the djs, the talk over traditions had always been partly rooted in the church, where "speaking out" and "bearing witness" are part of normal worship. Slack style undermined these traditions. In Seaga's Jamaica Inc, sex, money, flash and nonsense have tended to become the new religion of the airwaves. The new Jamaican djs like Ringo and Lone Ranger soon followed Yellowman with copycat "slack" tracks. It wasn't long before "slackness" was all the rage.

Dj take over

"Minuet oh vouty laho reetie o dingo reenie mo in oh vouty sow routie mo oh scoodly reenie mo."
(Slim Gaillard, US 1930s jive singer and inventor of the nonsense language, Vout*)*

As the 1980s progressed, the djs began to outstrip the singer-songwriters in popularity. Sound system culture began to take over more and more from "live" music as the place where Jamaican reggae was *really* happening. From the late 1970s onwards an army of djs had been competing for the fans' attention. New names appeared one week, only to be forgotten the next. Here are just some of them: Barrington Levy, U Brown, Jah Thomas, Lui Lepke, Charlie Chaplin, Captain Sinbad, Raymond Naptali, Burro Banton, Ranking Joe, Shadowman, Billy Boyo, Little Harry, El Fego Bacca, Peter Metro, Tony Tuff, Little John, Ranking Toyan and Outlaw Josey Wales. Some of these masters of the dance hall style rode out the competition. But the race was tough and many fell at the first fence. Some of the older "cultural" djs weathered the storm of slackness, though many others were edged out. And some simply left the field in disgust. One dj, Prince Far-I, was held in particular esteem as a kind of elder statesman until his untimely death in the wake of the elections.

Of the newer talk over artists one man literally towered head and shoulders above the rest. That was Ripton Hilton, the six-foot six-inch giant who calls himself Eek a Mouse after a comic book exclamation. Eek a Mouse is a complete one-off. He is the master of nonsense, reggae surrealism and word play. In songs like *Stadium Hot*, *The Mouse and the Man*, *Pretty City* and *The Lion Sleeps Tonight* he subjects the English language to a kind of comic massacre, stretching words into pure sounds and giving them new shapes as he sings the lyrics in his inimitable nasal whine. In some of his toasts (like *Hitler* and *Terrorists in the City*) Eek a Mouse offers a critical commentary on the politics of race, class, policing, and so on. But most of the time he doesn't try to make what the rest of us call sense at all:

> "She tek me by the hand
> And carry me to Disneyland
> Where I met Mickey Mouse
> I and Mickey both shake hands
> He is the mouse I am the man
> Bing bong diddy bay-o."

To see Eek a Mouse perform live is an experience you are unlikely to forget. When he strides on stage, larger and leaner than life, he is likely to be dressed up as some hero from fiction or mythology. One night it will be Robin Hood (his costume: a green hat with a feather in it, green tunic, pale green tights and bootees). Another night he will appear as Clint Eastwood (this time: an enormous sombrero, a giant poncho, skin-tight pants and boots with spurs). He will strike a pose under the lights, stand stock still for a few seconds, lower his forehead and stare straight into the crowd – a look of Spaghetti Western menace or Sherwood Forest dread on his face – and suddenly as the band begin to move off into the first thunderous reggae riff, he will start to sing . . . not in the gravelly Lee Marvin drawl you might expect from looking at the size of the man, but in a strange little strangulated voice pitched right up in the top of his head. Prowling back and forth from one end of the stage to the other on his endless legs, Eek a Mouse will run through his repertoire, freezing from time to time under the lights to pose for the audience or to glower at it after ordering his band to "DUB IT!" At other times, he will stand still – one hand on his hip – and call out to the crowd: "Ladies! I must ask you something! Do you LERVE Eek a Mouse?" He will then cup one enormous hand behind his ear in an exaggerated arc, listening for the affirmative response which more often than not is shouted back by the delighted fans.

Eek a Mouse has made a career out of playing on the contradiction between his size and shape and the pleasure he takes in being silly. A child-man, he laughs at himself and wins the audience over to his side by mixing verbal ingenuity with strong, danceable rhythms. Eek a Mouse is the court jester of reggae and, like the original court jesters in the Middle Ages, there is a satirical intention behind his "harmless" jokes. Because indirectly Eek a Mouse is getting us to laugh at the macho posturing which has been a major cause of so much pain and bloodshed in Jamaica in recent years. When we laugh at Eek a Mouse with his peculiar voice, his fancy dress and his silly rhymes, we are really laughing *with* him at the gangsters, the gunmen and the military goon squads. In fact we are laughing at all those people who take themselves too seriously. Eek a Mouse doesn't mind if we laugh, so long as we look and listen as he punctures the mystique of masculinity. And if Eek a Mouse represents the joyful, positive side of post-Seaga buffoonery then slackness represents the other nasty, fearful side. Because "slack style" talk over is based on a deep-seated distrust and fear of women. That is why women are reduced in slack mouth reggae to the status of cattle, dumb sex objects, and the butt of crude "humour".

But ultimately the retreat from protest and political commentary in Jamaican reggae into woman-hating jokes and slack mouth word play can't be blamed on Yellowman. He is more of a symptom than a cause. The shooting of Bob Marley in 1977 and the premature deaths of reggae artists like Mikey Smith, General Echo, Hugh Mandell and Prince Far-I during the Jamaican "troubles" were enough to discourage all but the bravest or most foolhardy performers from speaking out too loudly against Babylon. It is sad but true that right now the times seem to be just too dread for "truth and rights" in Jamaica.

There are also deeper reasons for the decline in Rasta-inspired reggae in the 1980s. By the late 1970s the music was starting to become predictable and closed in upon itself. The old Rasta chants were beginning to sound tired. This was because well before 1980 the obsession with roots had led to the growth of a kind of fundamentalism amongst some reggae fans, performers and pro-ducers. Just as fundamentalist Christians refuse to accept the need for change and new interpretations of what the Scriptures mean, so the roots reggae fundamentalists refused to tolerate new musical inputs. They would only allow experimentation in reggae within the narrow framework provided by "heavy" or "African" rhythms. By doing this they had turned their backs on the future and on growth. They had stripped the music down to its "purest" form, and in the process the music had begun to die. The answer had to be "cut 'n' mix". Reggae would only be renewed and refreshed if it was combined again with other forms of music. Ska had begun as a hybrid sound: a mix of r&b, mento, jazz, gospel, Pocomania and burra rhythms. And if it was to survive into the 1980s, Jamaican popular music would have to go back to its source in the mix. This was the lesson that a new generation of black British musicians was learning fast.

Chapter Fifteen

Lovers' rock: reggae, soul and broken hearts

"I grew up hearing the Supremes, Stevie Wonder, The Jacksons... Then there was Minnie Ripperton, Aretha (Franklin), so many. But *Catch a Fire* came out when I was still at school, and it really got to me – Bob Marley and the I-Threes. I really started listening and becoming aware of my roots, my culture, where I'm coming from and how I should be... [But] in Jamaica, it's always been *roots* and the men singing about their culture and Rasta. And because of that, women had a low profile."

(Caroll Thompson interviewed in 1985)

Reggae and other Caribbean sounds were not the only types of music available to young black Britons. Quite apart from Western classical music, pop, rock and so on, there was an enormous amount of black music to listen to. In the 1940s there had been blues, swing and bebop jazz. In the 1950s there had been hard bop, cool jazz and r&b. In the 1960s there was free form jazz and soul. And gospel, like the Church itself, was *always* there to be turned back to when people needed inspiration and support. By the 1970s and 1980s the record buyer faced an even wider choice. First there was a growing interest in the black musical heritage, so people were going back to all this earlier music. Then there was funk, African pop and jazz, West African Hi-Life, all kinds of Latin-influenced pop and salsa. And by now completely new types of music were available too – jazz-funk, hip hop, rap, duck rock, pop based on the African Burundi beat. The choice was overwhelming.

Some of these musics had been created by mixing together sounds and rhythms from different sources. When music from two or more sources is so completely blended that a new sound is created it is sometimes called *fusion* music. Jazz-funk is a good example of a fusion sound. In other cases, the different sounds are all jumbled up together but can still be traced back directly to their sources. Hip hop is a good example of this second type of music. In hip hop the hard funk beat stays the same throughout but the dj mixes in snatches of sound from other records. A hip hop record can contain recognisable snatches of hard rock, electro funk, salsa, soul, new wave, jazz, and so on. In fact a hip hop dj can pull in any sound, from a recording of a car screeching round a corner or a television news broadcast to Frank Sinatra singing *My Way*. It can all be added to the mix. What we get at the end of all this cutting and mixing is a kind of *mosaic* effect. Just as in a mosaic the overall pattern is made by placing little bits of differently coloured stone together, so hip hop is made by splicing together fragments of sound from quite different sources and traditions. And just as you can see the joins between the stones in a mosaic if you stand close enough, so you can hear the breaks and joins between the different sounds on a hip hop record if you listen carefully. In the next chapter, we shall return to hip hop and the relationship between this kind of music and the new British reggae.

Lovers' rock grew up in the 1970s and is more like a fusion sound than a mosaic.[1] Some music experts would argue that it is just another type of reggae. But Lovers' rock brings soul and reggae so close together that it really is a fusion of the two. To understand how this came about we have to look back at the London club scene in the mid-1970s. At this time, reggae and soul tended to be kept rigidly apart. Soul and reggae fans rarely mixed in the same clubs. They tended to dress, talk and dance differently. On the face of it, soul and reggae were about different things. While soul bands like Parliament, Funkadelic and Earth, Wind and Fire were playing with science fiction imagery and dressing up in glitter, reggae was going back to Africa, nature and the roots. The two types of music seemed to face in opposite directions. By the mid-1970s there was only one club in central London where roots reggae was played on a regular basis – the Roaring Twenties in Soho. Lloyd Coxsone was the man who operated the system, Sir Coxsone International. And to vary the tempo a little he decided to try something new. Coxsone began to play the odd soul record in between all the Marley and Big Youth tracks. Men and women could dance close to the slow, smoochy type of soul, so this kind of music became especially popular. One tune was soon a favourite with the crowd. This was *Caught in a Lie* by Donnie Elbert, and it became Coxsone's signature tune.

But it was Dennis Bovell who actually made the leap to Lovers' rock. Bovell was dj at the Metro club in West London. He was also a musician. He had co-founded the reggae group Matumbi in 1972. And he was also a record producer. Bovell was involved in some of the heaviest reggae going, but he didn't bother too much about "roots". He was more interested in cut 'n' mix. In fact, he went on to produce by himself an entire double album called *Brain Damage*, which was devoted to "mutant" reggae. (Mutant reggae is reggae which has been knocked into a different shape by banging up against calypso, r&b, rock 'n' roll, disco, etc.) When Coxsone suggested that he and Bovell might make a reggae version of *Caught in a Lie*, Bovell jumped at the idea. He had already spotted a thirteen-year-old singer called Louisa Mark, who had just the right kind of yearning voice that the song needed. The Louisa Mark version of *Caught in a Lie* was a hit with British reggae fans. It was one of the first records to break through the record buyers' prejudices against English reggae. Bovell went on to record other girl singers, discovering new talent by holding auditions every Sunday afternoon at the Eve studio in South London where he worked as an engineer. The first album in the new style was called *Love Affair* by Marie Pierre. Next Bovell went on to record girl *groups* like 15, 16 and 17, who had a reggae hit with *Black Skinned Boys*, and Brown Sugar, who recorded a song called *I'm in Love with a Dreadlocks*. It was around this time that Bovell began putting the Lovers' rock logo on the record labels, and the name soon began to catch on. A new type of reggae had arrived on the scene.

Louisa Mark followed up her early success with records like *All My Loving*, *Keep It As It Is*, *Reunited* and, her biggest hit to date, *Six Street*. And by the early 1980s, Lovers' rock had other established stars like Janet Kay, Jean Adebamba and Carroll Thompson. Jean Adebamba hit the reggae charts in 1981 with *Paradise*. Since then she has begun to add pepper to the Lovers' rock tradition by making political statements in her songs. In *English Girl*, for instance, the strong, sweet quality of her voice doesn't conceal the bitter message about British racism.

Janet Kay also found an audience *outside* the narrow reggae market. In 1979 she got to number two in the national charts with a song called *Silly Games*. Carroll Thompson established another first for women reggae singers in Britain by forming her own company, C&B, in 1981. In 1980 she recorded and produced her first hit album, *Hopelessly in Love*. Although it didn't get much airtime on the radio and never made the national charts, the album sold over 35,000 copies. Soon there were dozens of Lovers' rock singers like T. T. Ross, Black Harmony, Paulette Miller, Jennifer Daye, Yvonne Curtis, Sister C C, Samantha Rose, Sandra Reid, Sandra Williams, Cassandra, Phillis Wilson, Jackie Dale and Paulette Tajah. Gradually Lovers' rock matured into a recognisable style. One recording engineer described the style as "crisp and clean" vocals with a "round, flowing bass line" and plenty of strings and harmonies. And Lovers' rock sold records. In fact it outsold a lot of the heavy stuff. At one time in 1980, there were thirteen female Lovers' rock records in the *Black Echoes* Top 40.

Neither Janet Kay nor Carroll Thompson stayed just with Lovers' rock. Janet Kay still sings cover versions of reggae hits when she performs live, but as the 1980s have progressed she has moved closer and closer to soul and funk. Carroll Thompson has moved in a similar direction. She has joined the jazz-funk-pop band Floy Joy. And as a soloist she now records soulful ballads and soft funk along with Lovers' rock. But that move into soul can't be seen as a "sell out", because Lovers' rock had always been partly rooted in black American popular music. Janet Kay's very first record had been a Lovers' version of Minnie Ripperton's *Loving You*. So when she moved over fully into soul and funk she was in a sense coming home to her musical roots.

At its core, Lovers' rock has always been about romance and the pain of being in and out of love. It's sometimes criticised for not dealing with the "serious" issues. But this can be a bit puritanical. After all, for most music lovers, music is more to do with pleasure than education. And for most people the issues that Lovers' rock deals with *are* the serious issues. For Clem Bushay of Trojan Records, love is simply *the* vital issue. It sells records for a good reason:

> "I believe that there are more people in the world who are more concerned about love than anything else. Because it happens to them."[2]

In the end, though, Lovers' rock is important because it gave British black women a chance to make themselves heard in reggae music. It enabled women to develop the music in another direction. According to Jackie of Alpha, another Lovers' rock group:

> "For female British black reggae singers it's just the beginning. We're starting to come out – and we're very ambitious."[3]

And though Lovers' rock is often dismissed for putting women back into a dependent position, it's clear that not all Lovers' music is about crying over men. Jean Adebamba has added broad social comment and in 1984, The Wild Bunch released a song in the Lovers' style called *Indestructible Woman* with lines like this:

> "But you see me, I'm tough
> No man's going to hit me, I'm rough
> I'm an indestructible woman, and no man's gonna put me down."

Lovers' rock was not just confined to Britain. The sound and the name caught on in the Caribbean too, where it was applied to the more melodic reggae. For instance in Jamaica, Barbara Jones has produced some beautiful haunting songs in the Lovers' rock style, recording both original material and cover versions of old ballads. On the records she made in the late 1970s, her sad, yearning voice was often highlighted by the bare instrumental arrangement which framed it. The stripped down instrumental backing helped to conjure up a picture of the singer as an isolated figure in an empty room. On her version of the old Tin Pan Alley classic, *Send Me the Pillow that You Dream On*, the refrain that opens the song is played on a slightly out of tune piano, and this adds to the impression of loneliness and isolation. It is as if the singer has stayed on at a night club or a party after all the other people have left; she sounds far away like a voice in a dream. Later the piano is brought back in for a brief solo. We hear the faltering refrain once more as the notes tumble out against the steady, languorous rhythm of the reggae bass. It is as if the pianist is in a wistful mood and is trying to recall a favourite old melody. As the record draws to a close, Barbara Jones' voice is double-tracked so that a harmony is created. If she has been jilted, then she can at least console herself by singing a duet with her own voice.

Together, these sounds and effects provide the perfect atmosphere to complement the words of the song, which is about two lovers whose separation is so complete that the singer can only ask to share her former partner's dreams. By the closing bars, she sounds resigned to loneliness, but the longing is still there. And when the song is over it is the longing we are left with. That's what makes these songs so haunting. In this and in other original compositions like *Just a Friend*, Barbara Jones manages to move the listener without great displays of emotion. By subtly controlling her voice and by keeping it within a relatively narrow range, she conveys an impression of simplicity and artlessness. The effect can be striking. Sometimes she can sound like a schoolgirl in a playground singing along to her favourite record on the radio. And at her best, Barbara Jones can be the Billie Holliday of reggae music.

The Cool Ruler and Dennis Brown: men and Lovers' Rock

Just as the Lovers' rock tag wasn't attached only to British artists, so it wasn't just applied to female singers either. In Britain, the bridge between soul and reggae was also crossed by male singers like Trevor Walters, who recorded a reggae version of *Stuck on You* which went higher in the charts than Lionel Ritchie's original recording. And in Jamaica men had been singing romantic reggae songs since the days of Owen Gray, Alton Ellis and Ken Boothe. In the late 1970s the work of singers like Sugar Minott, Dennis Brown and Gregory Isaacs began to be classified as Lovers' rock too, though it bears little resemblance to the output of a Carroll Thompson or a Janet Kay. Minott and the rest are sometimes placed in the Lovers' category because their songs are about love and romance and because they have attracted huge followings of women fans. This was particularly true of Gregory Isaacs, the Cool Ruler in the late 1970s and early 1980s. Isaacs began his singing career in 1973 and has since produced a string of massive hits, alternating between love songs like *Extra Classic* and *Loving Pauper* and more Rasta-inspired material like *Slave Master* and *Black against Black*. The same mixture of the rough and the smooth was reflected in Isaacs' cool image. In "live" appearances he combined Rasta dreadlocks, expensively tailored three-piece suits and lots of gold jewellery. And his voice was as silky as the shirts he wore on stage. The combination of Isaacs' strong but gentle soulful voice and his elegant style at the microphone was irresistible. Whether pleading for his *Night Nurse* or sighing a farewell in *Sad to Know (you're leaving)*, Gregory Isaacs could wrap any listener round his little finger. And his reputation as a "badman" and a high liver off stage didn't do him any harm as far as most of his fans were concerned. It only enhanced his romantic appeal, especially when this reputation was laid against the vulnerable, lovelorn image he projected on vinyl. An Isaacs' album appeared in 1980 called *Lonely Lover* and that just about sums up the star's image.

One record, *The Border*, shows Gregory Isaacs at his best. To a fast stepping Rasta drum pattern backed by a chorus of horns, he sings the words:

> "If I could mek the border
> Then I would step across
> Simply tek me to the border
> No matter what's the cost
> Because I'm leavin' here
> I'm a leavin' outta Babylon
> I'm a leavin' outta Rome
> I'm a leavin' outta dis land
> Say me wan', me wan' go home
> Where the milk and honey flow
> Africa me wanna go."

The lyrics seem to suggest that this is yet another variation on the Back to Africa theme. But the way Isaacs handles the song colours the original meaning. His voice yearns beyond the "story" the song seems to be telling. *Border* isn't just about crossing from one country to another, from a place called Jamaica to a place called Africa. Isaac's desire to get across to the other side is so intense that the song begins to sound in places like a prayer. It mixes up the sense of loss and longing to such an extent that it's impossible to decide, when the record's over, whether you've been listening to an erotic song, a spiritual one, a mixture of the two or neither. With talent like that, it's a great pity that Gregory Isaacs doesn't seem to have "crossed over" into the second half of the decade. At one point in the early 1980s, he was arrested and imprisoned for possession of firearms. And there have been signs in recent years that Isaacs' fast lifestyle has at last begun to catch up with him. There are reports that his voice and his ability to perform have been affected by the way he has abused his body. The loss of a performer like Gregory Isaacs can only be another severe blow to Jamaican reggae music even if – as every reggae lover must surely hope – he manages to make a come-back some time in the future.

In Britain, Winston Reedy from North London has followed in the footsteps of the Cool Ruler. On his album *Dim the Light* he switches back and forth like Isaacs between melodic love songs and Rasta-influenced lyrics. And in Jamaica, Dennis Brown has served up the same menu in a series of hits and best-selling albums with titles like *Wolves and Leopards*, *If I Follow My Heart*, *Words of Wisdom* and *Revolution*. In fact, Brown has been linked to Lovers' rock right from the beginning. When he visited London in the mid-1970s, he used to stay with Dennis Bovell, and he even sang duets on stage with Louisa Mark before she made *Caught in a Lie*.

If anyone in Jamaica has inherited Isaacs' crown as leading male vocalist on the island then it is surely Dennis Brown. The two men adopt a similar style. Brown has a suit-and-dreadlocks image too. And in *Promised Land*, which he recorded with Aswad in 1984, he even develops a vocal style which is close, though not identical, to the one Isaacs uses on *The Border*. The two records work in a similar way though the instrumental backing on the Brown/Aswad cut is heavier and more centred round the bass. On this record, Brown's soaring vocals don't just talk *about* salvation. They *take* the listener on a journey over the border to the Promised Land.

But the Promised Land is a long way away from Lovers' rock. And it's stretching the label too far to try to stick it on records like this. Lovers' rock deals with the emotional problems we all face as we try to get through our ordinary lives. It doesn't concern itself with the big dreams and the Promised Land but with ordinary people's everyday desires and disappointments. And though there may be common bonds between the different kinds of yearning – the yearning for a lover and for deliverance from Babylon – those bonds are buried pretty deep. For, in the end, Lovers' rock was moving in another direction altogether. It wasn't off to Zion. If it was going anywhere at all, it was moving towards black urban America and soul music. What Lovers' rock did was to give young women a voice inside reggae without forcing them to deliver sermons when they didn't want to. It didn't ask them to lay down the law for the "righteous". In some cases, in records like *Indestructible Women*, it implied that all laws were made by men anyway and that women didn't have to bow down to any man-made laws unless they wanted to. Most importantly, Lovers' rock made it possible for women to sing about real things close to home – things that affected *them*. And to most black British girls living in places like Tottenham and Handsworth, Africa didn't look much like home. For behind the success and popularity of Lovers' rock among the female audience there was another message. The message was that the soul of the big American cities, of Aretha Franklin and Diana Ross and newer singers like Gwen Guthrie, was there to teach women about a different set of options. The message was that certain kinds of soul music might have more to offer the average young black British woman than all the "slackness" Yellowman could muster. Perhaps black women could get a more positive, modern and practical image for themselves from soul than they could from reggae with its Rasta rules about what women should be like, its covered locks and clouds of ganja smoke.

There was, of course, more than just one kind of soul music. It wasn't *all* smokey ballads and crystal clear vocals. Another strand within soul – the hard funk of people like James Brown, the JBs and Sly and The Family Stone – smudged the voice and stripped the beat down to the bone. This kind of music had its fans in Britain too. And the funk strand was getting a sharp new twist in America in the late 1970s at the hands of some of the djs. Before we turn to the fast style of the 1980s reggae MCs we have to make one last detour – this time to New York – to see how the mosaic of black American rap music was put together. Because fast style British reggae was heavily influenced by rap. Rap was one source of inspiration for the new MCs, just as Tamla Motown and Atlantic soul had been a source of inspiration for the British Lovers' rock singers. And to complete the circle, rap music, as we shall see, owed something to 1970s Jamaican talk over and dub.

Chapter Sixteen

Rap and hip hop: the New York connection

"I went into Body Music [a black owned record shop in Tottenham specialising in soul and reggae] the other day and asked for *The Lord's Prayer*. The guy serving sez: 'Certainly sir. Do you want it wrapped?'

I sez: 'Yes please.'

He sez [to a hip hop beat]:

'Our father which art up there, hallowed by Thy name.

Thy kingdom come, Thy will be done for ever more amen.' [pronounced ah-main!]."

(Joke told me by a white Tottenham reggae fan)

"Anybody who picks up the wax is a friend in my heart"

(Dj Kool Herc)

Rap is dj and MC music. Like talk over and toasted reggae it relies on pre-recorded sounds. In the case of rap the basic beat comes from hard funk rather than Jamaican rhythms, and it is true that there are important differences between rap and reggae. But the process leading to the production of dj reggae and rap is basically the same. The MCs "rap" – speak and in some cases half sing – their lines in time to rhythms taken from records. And the content of these raps is similar, too. There are boast raps, insult raps, news raps, "message" raps, nonsense raps, party raps and motherly or fatherly, sisterly or brotherly advice raps, just as there are in dj reggae. There are also other similarities. Just as reggae is bound up with the idea of roots and culture, so rap is rooted in the experience of lower class blacks in America's big northern cities.

The culture that grew up round rap is sometimes called "hip hop". Hip hop culture involves dance, dress, language and wild style graffiti. At its core it also involves an attitude. In the words of Afrika Bambaata, a leading hip hop dj: "It's about survival, economics and keeping our people moving on."[1] Rap did for poor blacks in America in the 1980s what reggae had done for the "sufferers" in Jamaica a decade earlier. It got them noticed again and it helped to forge a sense of identity and pride within the local community. Like reggae, the music later found an international audience. And then the sense of identity and pride that went along with rap became available to other people who listened to the music. The hip hop attitude and culture grew up with the music wherever rap was performed or played. By the 1980s hip hop began to receive a further boost with the release of films like *Wild Style* and *Beat Street*.

Both reggae and rap also grew out of city slum environments. Rap started in the South Bronx of New York, which had been a mainly black and Hispanic ghetto for decades. By 1930 nearly a quarter of the people who lived there were West Indian immigrants. And most of the Spanish speakers living in the Bronx nowadays either came originally from Caribbean islands like Puerto Rico and Cuba or are the children of Caribbean immigrants. The Cubans began arriving in the Bronx in the 1930s and 1940s and the Puerto Rican community goes back even further. There are now three million Puerto Ricans living in New York – as many as live in Puerto Rico itself. The Bronx had never been prosperous. But in the 1960s it went into a sudden decline and by the end of the decade it had become the poorest, toughest neighbourhood in the whole of New York City.

The beginning of hip hop

In 1967 a dj called Kool Herc emigrated to the States from Jamaica and came to live in the West Bronx. Herc knew the Jamaican sound system scene, and had heard the early talk overs of the new djs like U Roy. By 1973 Herc owned his own system. This was much louder and more powerful than other neighbourhood disco set-ups, and it had a much fuller and crisper sound. But when he began dee-jaying at house parties he found that the New York black crowd would not dance to reggae. So he began talking over the Latin-tinged funk that he knew *would* appeal. To start with he merely dropped in snatches of street slang, like the very first toaster djs who worked for Coxsone Dodd's system in the 1950s. He would shout phrases like "Rock on my mellow! This is the joint!". The talk was meant to keep the people dancing and to add the excitement that comes from "live" performance. Gradually he developed a style that was so popular that he began buying records for the instrumental breaks rather than for the whole track. The lead guitar or bass riff or sequence of drumming that he wanted might only last fifteen seconds. Rather than play the whole record straight through he would play this same part several times over, cutting from one record deck to the other as he talked through the microphone. This meant buying several copies of the same record. And it also meant that Herc had to have a very precise sense of timing. He used the headphones that djs use to cue up their records so that he could cut from one copy of a record to another at exactly the right point.

Kool Herc found that the drumming on a record called *Apache* by The Incredible Bongo Band was particularly suited to his needs. The Incredible Bongo Band were a Jamaican disco group and their version of *Apache* was released in 1974. But it had been written for the Shadows, Cliff Richard's backing group, in 1960. It had then been "covered" by an American group called The Ventures, who had a minor hit with it in the States. The Incredible Bongo Band used conga drums instead of the standard pop music drum kit. And they laid more stress on the percussion. Thanks to Kool Herc, *Apache* could be heard all over the Bronx in 1975.

The style Herc had invented became known as the "beats" or the "break-beats". And he can be credited with another first. As the switching between record decks got faster and more complicated it required a lot of concentration. Herc couldn't "rap" and operate the records at the same time. So he employed two MCs, Coke-la-Rock and Clark Kent, to do the rapping for him. The MCs would put on a show for the crowd, dancing in front of the decks and bouncing lines off each other. The first MC dance team had arrived.

Soon other djs began copying Herc's style and adding their own refinements. A dj called Theodor invented a technique called "scratching". This involves spinning a record backwards and forwards very fast while the needle is in the groove. When handled in this way, a record can be turned into a percussive instrument. Scratching was used to foreground the beat even further.

Grandmaster Flash (Joseph Saddler) was another Bronx dj who helped to create the hip hop style. His parents came from Barbados and his father had a big collection of Caribbean and black American records. Flash was fascinated not just by the music but by the records themselves. For him they were things to be looked at, touched and handled, not just played:

> "My father was a very heavy record collector. He still thinks that he has the stronger collection. I used to open his closets and just watch all the records he had. I used to get into trouble for touching his records, but I'd go right back and bother them."[2]

After graduating in electronics, Flash began combining his two main interests: sound techology and hard funk. He made his own system and would play at night in local parks. To get the power he needed to operate the system he would run a cable from the decks and amplifier to the nearest street light. Flash became an expert at *punch phasing*.

This is when the dj hits a particular break on one deck while the record on the other turntable is still playing. The punch works in hip hop like a punctuation mark in a sentence. It helps to give shape to the flow of sounds on the record in the same way that a comma or a full stop helps to shape the flow of written language. And just as punctuation brings time to the pages of this book by telling the reader when to pause, so the punch in hip hop can be used to accentuate the beat and the rhythm for the dancing crowd. Flash was also one of the first hip hop djs to work with a beat box: a machine that produces an electronic drum beat. Together with his MC crew – headed in those days by Melle Mel – Grandmaster Flash and the Furious Five produced a hard rapping style which became their trademark. As Flash leapt from deck to deck using multiple turntables Mel would rap in an aggressive, staccato style to the raw, stripped down electronic beat:

> "Rappin' on the mike, makin' cold, cold cash
> With a joker spinnin' for me called DJ Flash."[3]

Afrika Bambaata was another major figure right from the early days. He ran a sound system at the Bronx River Community Center. Today he is a figurehead for hip hop. He acts as an ambassador and spokesman for the music and its culture, just as Bob Marley did for reggae. Afrika Bambaata is the name of a famous nineteenth-century Zulu Chief; it means "Affectionate Leader". And Bambaata takes this role seriously. In 1975 he started an organisation for funk loving street kids, later known as the Zulu Nation. Bambaata based his Nation on the idea of the Zulu military system, and tried to adapt the structure of the black New York street gangs accordingly. Bambaata had himself been a member of the Black Spades – New York's biggest black gang in the 1960s and early 1970s. But he had seen how violence and heroin had destroyed the gangs. In the Zulu Nation he set out to replace "rumbles" (fights) and drugs with rap, dance and hip hop style. He wanted to turn the gang structure into a positive force in the ghetto. Bambaata's dream is that a sense of community can be created *within* the community rather than being imposed by people coming from outside. He believes that through organisations like the Zulu Nation the people at the bottom of society will learn how to help themselves and each other.

This vision is not unlike Marley's (or Manley's, for that matter). Bambaata became interested in the politics of race and culture through the Black Muslims, a militant black sect. During the 1960s the Black Muslims won many converts, including Cassius Clay – Mohammed Ali, the great boxing champion. They helped to create a new mood of confidence in the black ghettoes of the Western world.

The Black Muslims talked about the need for self-help and communal solidarity. And Bambaata wanted to link music up to the issues the Muslims were raising. We have seen how Bob Marley had helped to steer reggae music through the rude boy era towards the Rastafarian themes of roots and culture. And at about the same time, Bambaata was trying to guide black street kids through the gang phase towards a sense of collective solidarity and a more constructive attitude. By the early 1980s, the Zulu Nation had thousands of members worldwide.

By this time a style had grown up round hip hop. Crews of break-dancers (called B-boys and B-girls) had developed acrobatic dance routines which stretch the human body to its limits. First there was the Floor Lock. In this move, the dancers support themselves on one hand while spinning their bodies round and kicking out their legs. Then other moves were added. There was the Handglide or Flow (spinning while balanced on one elbow).[4] There was the Backspin, the Headspin, the Windmill (using the shoulders as the pivot). There was Lofting (diving in the air and landing on the hands). And once you had committed a Suicide (fallen forward with the hands at the sides and landed flat on your back) you could (if you were still alive!) freeze into a posture which told the crowd that the routine was over. Then there was another set of dance moves sometimes called "electric boogie". These include the Tick, the Mannequin or Robot, the King Tut, the Wave and the Pop, the Float and the Moonwalk glide. All these moves require the dancer to snap and twitch muscles in time to the music in a highly disciplined way. The Lock It is a dance mime version of laughing (slapping hands on the knees, etc.). Then there is "uprock", which is a fighting dance based loosely on kung fu moves. And around 1982 "freestyle" came in. As the name suggests freestyle leaves the B-girl or B-boy to improvise like the jazz dancers of the 1940s bebop era. Rival dance crews fight dancing duels drawing on these different dance styles. The aim is to burn off the opposition by suddenly performing an Unnamed Move (a move that hasn't been seen before and so can't be matched straightaway).

Obviously the emphasis on dancing influenced the dress. The clothes worn by B-dancers had to be comfortable, and washable. There could be nothing stiff or formal about them. So they started combining casual clothes and sportswear. After all, break-dancing, body popping and uprock are just as much athletic and competitive sports as baseball or football. The early B-style consisted of anoraks and sweatshirts with hoods, bellbottom jeans, tennis shoes and white sailors' caps with the brim sticking straight out in front. Later the style was modified: in came straight leg jeans, leather jerkins and bomber jackets, sweat shirts and trainers. Caps were worn back to front and on the back of the head.

The wild style graffiti had grown out of the fad among street gangs for "scribbling" their gang names on walls. In the hip hop era this became an art form in its own right. Individual artists used magic markers and spray paint to scribble their "tags" (nicknames) on every surface they could find. Subway trains were a favourite target. Soon the grey carriages of the New York underground system were lost beneath a wild riot of dayglo colours and ornate script. Some graffiti art is now so highly prized that it's sold for thousands of dollars in the New York galleries.

Beat and voice: the vital mix

At the centre of the hip hop culture was audio tape and raw vinyl. The radio was only important as a source of sounds to be taped. The break-dancers associated the black radio stations with disco: this was seen as the "official" black music of the mid to late 1970s. The hip hoppers "stole" music off air and cut it up. Then they broke it down into its component parts and remixed it on tape. By doing this they were breaking the law of copyright. But the cut 'n' mix attitude was that no one owns a rhythm or a sound. You just borrow it, use it and give it back to the people in a slightly different form. To use the language of Jamaican reggae and dub, you just *version* it. And anyone can do a "version". All you need is a cassette taperecorder, a cassette, a pair of hands and ears and some imagination. The heart of hip hop is in the cassette recorder, the drum machine, the Walkman and the big portable – (well, just about!) – ghetto blasters. These are the machines that can be used to take the sounds out on to the streets and the vacant lots, and into the parks.

It wasn't that the break-dancers didn't like artists like James Brown, Chic or Hamilton Bohannon, who got played on the black radio stations. Because they *loved* the funk these people played. And funk rhythm is the backbone of hip hop culture. It was just that the black street kids wanted to bypass the retail outlets. They wanted to undermine the system that had taken artists like James Brown from the ghetto and put them up there out of reach with all the other show business stars. By taping bits of funk off air and recycling it, the break-dancers were setting up a direct line to their culture heroes. They were cutting out the middlemen. And anyway, who *invented* music in the first place? Who ever *owned* sound and speech?

James Brown, the godfather of funk, gave his seal of approval to hip hop culture in 1984. He joined forces with Bambaata in that year to make a six-part rap record called *Unity* – a plea for peace ("We must push the button for life [the record button on a cassette machine] and nothing else"). And Brown had even hinted at the hip hop option in an old-style rap record called *Get Up, Get Into It, Get Involved* which he'd released way back in 1970:

> "You can be like a tape deck, you know
> They can plug you in.
> Say what you wanna say
> Don't let them do it."[5]

But it wasn't long before the hip hop sound could be heard on the radio, and eventually it was itself recorded on vinyl. In 1979 two rap records appeared from nowhere. First there was *King Tim 111 (Personality Jock)* by Fatback, a Brooklyn-based funk band. This was followed by *Rapper's Delight* by the Sugar Hill Gang. The second record was closer to the Bronx style and it crept into the bottom of the US Top 40. It later became an international hit. A flood of rap records followed, although it was some time before the *originators* of the hip hop style got into the studio.

In the early 1980s, Grandmaster Flash and the Furious Five released two classic hard hip hop hits: *Adventures of Grandmaster Flash And The Furious Five On The Wheels Of Steel* and *The Message*. The first record is an extraordinary adventure in itself. It is so raw and the cuts are so violent that it sounds more live than a live performance by a punk band. And yet it is built entirely out of second-hand materials. The record is a startling mix of different sounds: the bass line from the rock group Queen's 1980 hit *Another One Bites The Dust* is mixed with a riff from *Good Times*, Chic's disco hit from 1979. These are then mixed with snatches from four or five other rap records. Finally, towards the end of the record, a man and a young child read out extracts from an incomprehensible fairy story. All this is jumbled up and scratched together. The record is full of breaks and silences. But it is held together by the stuttering rhythm. Flash keeps holding the needle back, tearing great empty holes in the web of sound. But however long he waits, he always comes back to hit the mix with the right sound at the right time. He never misses the beat. And some of the sounds he "quotes" are really risky. At one point he mixes in a snatch of Latin salsa. The screaming horns and the eight-bar beat jar against the steady 4/4 time of the Queen bass. And yet somehow it works beautifully. *Adventures On The Wheels Of Steel* is an electro boast. Flash is challenging any other hip hop dj to a cut 'n' mix contest. He knows in his bones he can "flash fastest". The record is about taking sound to the very edge of chaos and pulling it back from the brink at the very last millisecond. On this record Flash is playing chicken with a stylus.

Grandmaster Flash's second classic rap single, *The Message*, plays the same game. Only this time the edginess is in the rap itself. The rhythm is much slower, moodier and steadier than on the earlier release. As the beat pulses along, a synthesizer trips gently up and down the scales in time to the beat. Four beats up, four straight beats. Four beats down, four straight beats. At the beginning of the record this is fine. It's a relief from the pared-down percussion. And it sounds quite lighthearted and playful. But it goes on and on. The beat becomes a kind of metaphor for being locked up. It's as if you're having to live for as long as the record lasts in a space as cramped as a South Bronx tenement. It's like hearing somebody drumming their fingers on a table as you're trying to read. By the end of the record the synthesizer tripping up and down the scales is beginning to sound like somebody running a stick along a railing or a metal mug along the bars of a prison window. Suddenly the hypnotic beat is joined by a man's voice. The voice mutters right up against your ear: "It's like a jungle sometimes/Sometimes I wonder how I keep from going under." This is repeated once and then the voice launches into a syncopated rap on the theme of living in a tenement slum. The voice conjures up vivid, sour images: broken glass is everywhere (there is the sound of a bottle breaking in the background). The voice tells us a story about a crazy bag lady living in the street. Then we get another story about a girl falling in front of a train, losing an arm and having it sewn on again. None of these bits and pieces add up to anything much. Sometimes the voice starts rapping about the pressure of living as a poor black in America:

"You gotta have money, ain't a damn thing funny
You gotta have a car in this land of milk and honey."

There's nothing stable or coherent in the world this record creates for us. The only constant is the menacing pulse of the beat with the stick being run up and down, up and down along the bars. At regular intervals the voice moves down into a brooding register and barks out the following lines, dropping each syllable like a bomb on the beat:

"Don't push me 'cos I'm close to the edge
I'm tryin' hard not to lose my head
It's like a jungle some times
Sometimes I wonder how I keep from going under."

This sequence is repeated a few times. Each sequence contains a different story. At the end of each story, the voice returns us to the edge.

Then suddenly the record launches into the main narrative. At last we get the message of the song. This time the story is all too coherent. The sequence of events it describes has a horribly inevitable feel about it. The message tells how a young boy living in a ghetto drifts out of school and into crime, gets an eight-year prison sentence for armed robbery, is sexually assaulted by older prisoners and ends up hanging himself in his cell. The message is directed at the listener, who is addressed as the young boy in the story. It's as though we are listening to the voice of someone talking to the corpse or the ghost of his younger brother. The message is: "don't hero worship gangsters or get involved in crime". The rap ends with the lines which started the song as the unremitting beat fades out into silence. *The Message* is a study in mood creation. The flat voice and thudding beat together take the listener across the border into a cold, bleak landscape. This time we are not being led to the Promised Land by Dennis Brown and Aswad. This time we are being led by the ears into hell. But what is so disconcerting and extraordinary about this record is that it mixes its moral with a slinky beat which is as irresistible to dance to as Sly Stone's *I Wanna Thank You (for letting me be myself)*.

Afrika Bambaata likes mixing things up, too. He has been known to cut from salsa to Beethoven's Fifth Symphony to Yellow Magic Orchestra to calypso through Kraftwerk via video game sound effects and the *Munsters* television series' theme tune back to his base in James Brown. And in 1982 he made a record with the Soul Sonic Force called *Planet Rock* which was a big hit. In its own way, *Planet Rock* is as bizarre as *Adventures On The Wheels Of Steel*. But the Soul Sonic Force didn't use the edgy staccato rapping style of The Furious Five. Instead their voices weave in and out of the pulsing party beat with lines like "More bounce to the ounce" and "Planet Rock. It just don't stop it's gonna drive you nuts!" Meanwhile Bambaata mixes in snatches of song and sound effects round the steady electronic beat. The rhythm of a rap record by Captain Sky called *Super Sporm* is crossed with the computer-generated rhythms and melodies of records like *Trans-Europe Express* and *Numbers* by the German electro group, Kraftwerk. This is then mixed up with the theme from the Clint Eastwood Spaghetti Western *For a Few Dollars More*. (The Eastwood themes composed by Ennio Morricone had also made a powerful impact on dub producers like Lee "Scratch" Perry in Jamaica in the 1970s.)

The daring of Bambaata's mixes and the black political input that he has made into hip hop have inspired other artists. Air Force One built a hip hop record round Ronald Reagan's famous gaffe when he made a "joke" at a TV station. Reagan had claimed in jest that he had the solution to the Russian "problem". "Ladies and gentlemen, fellow Americans," he says, barely able to restrain the laughter, "We begin bombing in five minutes." President Reagan was unaware that he was being recorded at the time. *See the Light, Feel the Heat* begins with Reagan's "announcement". The phrase "We begin bombing" is picked out and repeated several times as the funk rhythm breaks and crashes in a series of explosions round Reagan's voice. And each time the phrase comes back into the mix, the voice has become more distorted. Reagan's little "joke" gets less and less funny each time it's relayed. By using tape loops, echoes and breaks, by speeding up and slowing down the tape, Air Force One make a political statement without having to say anything directly. This technique has been used on many other records to undermine the official voices of authority. It has even been used in Britain by "scratch" video artists. People like the Duvet Brothers and George Barker tape television programmes – including news reports – off air, using domestic video cassette recorders. By re-editing the extracts, they change the meaning of what people in power think they're saying.

In a more respectful vein, the words of 1960s black leaders have been recycled in rap and soul. The voices of Martin Luther King, the Civil Rights leader, and Malcom X, spokesman for the Black Muslims, have both been brought back from the grave in this way. In *No Sell Out*, for instance, on Tommy Boy records, Malcom X's voice is heard "testifying" for the black experience in urban America in lines like: "The only thing that power respects *is* power . . . There will be no flim-flam, no sell out." Malcom X's hard, no-nonsense style of delivery fits the funk beat perfectly. This is no coincidence. When Malcom X was alive and making speeches, he drew on the rapping traditions in black street culture, jive and jazz. Malcom X's widow, Mrs Betty Shabazz, is aware of her late husband's connection to the rhythms of the street. And she gave her permission for Keith LeBlanc to use her late husband's voice on *No Sell Out*. It was Bambaata who paved the way for that connection between the street, black politics and the studio to be opened up again in the 1980s.

Malcolm McLaren, who managed the British punk group The Sex Pistols in the 1970s, has called *Planet Rock* "the rootsiest folk music around".[6] And though they may seem poles apart, Bambaata and McLaren share a lot of common ground musically. They both wage war on people's prejudices about popular music. In 1982, McLaren made an album called *Duck Rock* which used rap, African Zulu, Latin and Burundi rhythms, bits of patter recorded off radio and Appallachian hillbilly music. In his turn, Bambaata took inspiration and musical ideas from white punk and new wave music. He would mix up the theme from *The Pink Panther* with fragments from The Beatles, The Monkees and the Rolling Stones to create a dance beat that sounded like solid black funk. His aim was to get people to dance their way beyond their own prejudices. Jerry Dammers expressed a similar attitude in 1980 when he produced the album *More Specials*, which included muzak:

> "I listen to anything basically... it doesn't matter how good or bad it is, if you listen to it enough, you learn to like it. There's no such thing as good or bad music. I'd really like to destroy people's ideas of good and bad music so that eventually people will hear a record and they won't even know if they like it or not. That's my ambition..."[7]

And Horace Gentleman backed up Dammers' decision to move away from ska to draw on other musics:

> "What we came up with [on *More Specials*] is the songs side and the muzak side – the aim was to make it more international".[8]

When taken to its logical conclusion in rap, cut 'n' mix suggests that we shouldn't be so concerned about where a sound comes from. It's there for everyone to use. And every time a new connection is made between different kinds of music, a new channel of communication opens up.

The connections between rap and Caribbean music didn't have to be forced. A high proportion of the black population in the Bronx came originally from the West Indies. The area has its Puerto Rican and Cuban communities, too. And when these people came from the Caribbean, they brought their own music with them.[9] The streets of the South Bronx had been throbbing to the African-based Latin rhythms of the Cuban rumba, the mamba and the cha-cha-cha for decades. The Puerto Rican "danzon", which is based on European violin music, faded away when it was transplanted to New York. But the *plena*, with its African shuffle rhythm, survived and flourished. These Latin rhythms were sometimes blended with black American music. For instance in the 1960s there was a craze in New York for Latin soul. And the heavy funk beat of hip hop is regularly lifted by a dash of uptempo salsa. Salsa means "sauce" in Spanish, and it was South American listeners who first used the term to refer to New York Latin music in the 1940s and 1950s. Tito Puente, the great salsa percussionist and band leader, produces his own brand of the music, which draws on santeria rhythms. Puente is himself a priest of the Santeria faith. And now the Bronx throbs to the sound of the Santeria drums as well as the salsa protest songs of Ruben Blades from Panama and Celia Cruz, the Cuban "queen of salsa".

As we have seen, there is a reggae-rap connection through dj Kool Herc. And rap got exported back to Jamaica, too. Joe Gibbs cut a version of *Rapper's Delight* in 1979. On one side of the record, a duo called Xanadu and Sweet Lady rap the song New York fashion. On the other side, *Rocker's Choice*, they toast it Trenchtown style. And rap and reggae have a common root in a record called *Love is Strange* by Mickey and Sylvia. This record was released in 1956 at the time when ska and soul and rock 'n' roll were just beginning. On this record, guitarist Mickey Baker and vocalist Sylvia Vanderpool sing a bantering duet over a lilting Caribbean-flavoured shuffle rhythm. In the middle there is a sort of mini-rap between the two. Mickey asks Sylvia how she calls her lover boy. As Mickey keeps asking the question: "And if he *still* doesn't answer?", Sylvia calls back to him in a voice that gets sexier and sexier. The record made the top twenty in the States. It was a hit in Jamaica too. It is sometimes classified as a "rhythm and blues calypso hit".[10] And almost a quarter of a century later, it was Sylvia Vanderpool who set up Sugarhill Records with her husband. This was the company that released the first Bronx-style rap by the Sugarhill Gang before going on to record Grandmaster Flash and the Furious Five.

Some of the other strands that were woven into rap went into the making of reggae as well. David Toop has done some extraordinary detective work on where New York rap came from:

> "Rap's forebears stretch back through disco, street funk, radio djs, Bo Diddley, the be-bop singers, Cab Calloway, Pigmeat Markham, the tap dancers and comics, the Last Poets, Gil Scott-Heron, Muhammad Ali, acappella and doo-wop groups, ring games, skip rope rhymes, prison and army songs, toasts, signifying and the dozens, all the way back to the griots of Nigeria and Gambia."[11]

The mix is very rich. The radio djs Toop refers to were the jive-talkers of the be-bop era like Daddy O Daylie, Dr Hep Cat and Douglas Jocko Henderson (the "Ace from Space"). These djs used the human voice as an instrument so that the rhythm and sound of the words became more important than their meanings. As far as the early sound system operators in Jamaica were concerned, the patter of the djs was as important as the records they played. The first recorded toasts, like Sir Lord Comic's *Ska-ing West*, used the jive slang of the American radio djs, and U Roy released a record called *Your Ace From Space* no doubt in tribute to Jocko Henderson. Bo Diddley was famous for one record – an r&b boast song called *Bo Diddley* which he recorded in 1955. The song has a strong African beat which is made even more pronounced by the maraccas in the background. It is based on a rhythm sometimes called the "postman's knock" which was later used by Johnny Otis on *Willie and the Hand Jive* and by the Rolling Stones on *Not Fade Away*. Diddley calls out the boasts over this rhythm while the backing singers sing out the line "Hey, Bo Diddley". And it was this kind of raw, shuffle-rhythmed r&b that the sound system operators were playing in the Jamaican yards in the 1950s. In the 1930s and 1940s jazz bandleaders like Cab Calloway and singers like Slim Gaillard had invented nonsense languages. They got the audiences to join in by singing out lines which the crowd chanted back. You can hear the same silly call and response routines whenever Eek a Mouse takes the stage today.

Acappella just means "without instruments". In America in the 1950s there were literally hundreds of black street corner groups who tried to follow the success of doo-wop stars like The Platters. And soon there was a spate of vocal harmony groups in Jamaica too. (The voice is an instrument *everyone* can afford!) First there were the duos like Higgs and Wilson, and Jackie and Roy. In the late 1950s a Jamaican group called the Jivin' Juniors had an r&b hit with a record called *Sweet as an Angel*. And the vocal harmonies of groups like the Wailers had their roots in the same tradition.

Finally there were the old word games called "signifying" and the "dozens" in the States. These can be traced back to the West African roots and the griots. And versions of these boasting, insult and trickster games are played throughout the Caribbean. Always the vital mix is voice and rhythm. This is the mix that binds communities together across continents. And it's true even when the rhythms come out of a Roland TR 808 computerised drum machine. In the end it doesn't matter whether the voices are singing or shouting, rapping or toasting. They can be interrupted by video game bleeps and out-takes from Ronald Reagan speeches, and it still doesn't matter. Even when the vocalist is talking fast-style on a microphone in London about something called the *Cockney Translation*, the vital mix survives.

Chapter Seventeen

Fast-style reggae: designer label roots

> "With the Saxon Posse now, we chat what's happening here, not Jamaica, America or Timbuktu."
>
> *(Daddy Colonel)*

> "Sweet as a nut – just level vibes. Seen?"
>
> *(Smiley Culture)*

In 1984, Dub Vendor released a dj reggae record entitled *Cockney Translation* on the Fashion label. The record seemed to strike a chord with reggae fans. It went to number one in the British reggae charts and it stayed there for weeks. The MC on this record was Smiley Culture (David Emmanuel), a twenty-one-year-old from South London. Smiley's mother had come to Britain from South America and his Jamaican father has since moved to New York. Smiley himself was born in London. And *Cockney Translation* really takes the story from there:

> "11, 10, 9, 8, 7, 6, 5, 4, 3, 2, 1.
> It's Smiley Culture with the mike in a me hand
> Me come to teach you right and not the wrong
> In a de Cockney Translation.
>
> Cockney's not a language, it's only a slang
> And was originated yah so inna England
> The first place it was used was over East London
> It was respect for the different style pronounciation
> But it wasn't really used by any and any man
> Me say strictly con-man also the villain
> But through me fill up of lyrics and education
> Right here now you a go get a little translation.
>
> Cockney have names like Terry, Arthur and Del-Boy
> We have names like Winston, Lloyd and Leroy
> We bawl out YOW! While cockneys say Oi!
> What cockney call a Jack's we call a Blue Bwoy
> Say cockney have mates while we have spar
> Cockney live in a drum while we live in a yard
> Say we get nyam while cockney get capture

Cockney say Guv'nor, We say Big Bout Ya
In a de Cockney Translation!
In a de Cockney Translation!

Well watch a man
The translation of cockney to understand is easy
So long as you don't deaf and you listen to me keenly
You should pick it up like a youth who find some money
Go tell it to your friends also your family
No matter if a English or a Yardy
Ca' you never know when them might buck up a cockney
Remember warn dem dem deh man dem don't easy
Dem no fire sling shot a me say strictly double B
Dem run protection racket and control 'nuff C.I.D.

Say cockney fire shooter. We bus' gun
Cockney say tea leaf. We just say sticks man
You know dem have wedge while we have corn
Say cockney say Be first, my son! We just say Gwan!
Cockney say grass. We say outformer man
When dem talk 'bout iron dem really mean batty man
Rope chain and choparita me say cockney call tom
Say cockney say Old Bill. We say dutty Babylon
In a de Cockney Translation
In a de Cockney Translation.

But sometimes me shake out and leave me home town
And that's when me travel a East London
Where I have to speak as a different man
So that the cockney can understand
So black man and white man hear dem fashion

Cockney say scarper. We say scatter
Cockney say rabbit. We chatter
We say bleach. Cockney knackered
Cockney say t'riffic. We say waaacked!

Cockney say blokes. We say guys
Cockney say Alright? We say Ites!
We say pants. Cockney say strides
Sweet as a nut . . . just level vibes. Seen?"

Smiley Culture is part of a new generation of young black British
MCs who are talking their way into a new sound and a new identity.[1]
Cockney Translation is about this process. It's a joke *about* sounds
(slang and patois) and identities (being a cockney or a yardy). In the
record, Smiley Culture seems to be two separate people. Although he

is a Londoner he is also a *black* Londoner. He isn't a white, working-class cockney. But he isn't a rootsy Jamaican "yardy" either. He can speak both languages – Jamaican patois and cockney rhyming slang – but he doesn't fully *belong* in either camp. Like Anansi, the trickster spider, or Charles Dickens' Artful Dodger, he hops back and forth between the two roles when he needs to in order to keep out of trouble and earn a living.

On the *Cockney Translation* twelve-inch record sleeve there is a photograph of Smiley leaning against a car (a Nova Automatic) in a typical South London street (it looks like a lock-up under a railway bridge). The car has the figure 490 stuck on the windscreen and another sign in the background says ACCESS, BARCLAYCARD, VISA. Smiley himself is wearing a beret, a sheepskin coat and lots of "tom" (jewellery). There is a signet ring on every finger of his left hand and he has two gold "rope chains" hanging round his neck. The whole cover looks like a cheap advertisement for the kind of second hand car business that Arthur Daley might visit in the television series *Minder*. Smiley is looking straight into the camera as if to say would you buy a second hand car from someone like me? In other words, "do you trust me?" He is playing at being the cockney "con-man" and "villain". (In fact, in real life Smiley used to be an agent for a second hand car dealer.) But when the record was re-issued it included a bonus track called *Roots Reality*. The image seems to say this boy is only interested in getting your "'wedge" (money) out of your pocket and into his. But it's clear that with the new young British reggae MCs like Smiley Culture, questions of identity and culture are absolutely crucial.

Cockney Translation is fast-style reggae. Fast-style can be seen as reggae's answer to rap. The "solid" bass and drum foundation of "classical" reggae disappears as the new MCs reel off their lines to the light, tight beat pushed out by a drum machine. There are none of the echoing spaces and wierd effects of heavy dub. Fast-style doesn't seem to fit very neatly into the picture of reggae I presented in the earlier part of this book. The contrast with the heavy stuff could hardly be more underlined. Where reggae got slower, fast-style speeds up. Listening to a Lee Perry dub from the mid to late 1970s is like walking into a hall of mirrors or one of those crooked houses at the funfair where the perspectives don't add up. In the same way, the dimensions in a Perry dub record keep changing. You can never touch down and get your bearings. Fast-style is the opposite to that. On a fast-style toast you are taken on a headlong rush in one direction. Instead of shuffling round the crooked house of dub, it's like running through an ultra-modern maisonette where all the surfaces are clean and shiny.

Fast-style is associated with the Saxon International Sound System, which is based in Deptford in South London. It's run by Dennis Rowe and Lloyd Francis. (Dub Vendor, on the other hand, is run by two white ex-skinheads, Chris Lane and John MacGillivray.) Other MCs linked to the Saxon system include Tipper Irie, Daddy Colonel, Philip Levi, Asher Senator, Lady Di and Sister C. Peter King, who also worked for Saxon, was the first to use the style. But it was Philip Levi who first put speed reggae rapping on record in *Mi God Mi King*. (A history of fast-style is available on vinyl in Asher Senator's *Fast Style Origination*.) Soon the Rasta themes began to fall away, along with the booming bass and the spacey drum work. Instead of just "chatting 'pon a soun" and trusting Jah to help them find the right words, the MCs began writing down their lines beforehand and memorising them. In this way, it became possible for the MCs to develop more complex story-lines, drawing on their everyday experience. In Smiley Culture's follow-up to *Cockney Translation,* for instance, he uses the same two voices again. On *Police Officer* the cockney voice belongs to the police officer of the title. The yardy voice belongs to Smiley-the-reggae-superstar who's been stopped by the police officer while driving round London – an all too familiar experience for many young black British drivers. (As Ranking Ann says: "So you better watch out if you poor or you black/You drive your car you bound fe get stop.") The two voices argue with Smiley, pleading with the officer not to give him a "producer" (a demand to produce his driving licence at a police station within a specified period). Finally the argument is settled. The officer recognises Smiley as the star who produced *Cockney Translation*. Smiley gets his freedom in exchange for an autograph. *Police Officer* got to number twelve in the national charts. Its success was partly due to the refreshingly straightforward video which came out with the record. (The video cost £1,500 to make instead of the £20,000 which was what it cost to make the average pop or rock video promo at the time.)

Tipper Irie used a similar technique on *Complain Neighbour*. This time the cockneys are living next door to a noisy reggae blues party. (Tipper Irie's father ran a blues when Tipper was a nipper. He grew up like Grandmaster Flash surrounded by his father's records.) And there have been other MC comedy releases like Laurel and Hardy's *You're nicked* and *Eastenders* by Surgion and Herbtree. In this second record, the two MCs discuss and act out imaginary scenes from Britain's most popular television soap opera (which is set – like all these records – in a mythical place called Cockney Land).

Fast-style appealed to the young, sharp reggae fans living in London. It offered an image that seemed to fit life in the big city in

Mrs Thatcher's 1980s. It appealed to people who had been born in Britain and who feel that *this* is where they live and this is where they're going to stay. Unlike heavy reggae, rockers and steppers, it didn't just appeal to the boys. The Saxon Sound had begun as a Lover' rock system in 1976. And the female crowd have stayed with it because there's no slackness with Saxon and no macho rebel posing either. This doesn't mean that the pressure has lifted for black Londoners. Far from it. Unemployment is higher than ever. In many parts of London relations with the police have reached an all-time low. But the fast-style MCs have shown that anger is not the only resource black people have to draw upon. And for the new generation of young black Britons the right to feel relaxed and at home on Britain's streets is not a silly pipe dream. It is *the* political issue for black youth in the UK in 1986.

Fast-style grew up in the 1980s along with the fashion among British street kids for casual clothes and designer label sportswear. Although it began with the football-and-soul crowd in the late 1970s, the taste for expensive brand name clothes soon spread. By the early 1980s, the style of the racially mixed inner city areas was "casual". Sergio Tacchini tracksuits were worn with Adidas training shoes, Lacoste, Dior and Fred Perry tennis shirts, gold chains, bracelets, rings (and sometimes gold teeth!). The whole style looked cool and relaxed. It combined comfort and status. And it cut across racial lines. With the casual look, it didn't matter where your parents came from. What mattered was the pedigree of the clothes you wore. It sounds elitist. But in fact the style and the music that went with it (some soul, reggae, pop, jazz and rock) helped to create a common culture among inner city youths who lived next door to each other, and went to the same schools. As often as not they had to do the same kinds of casual work or cope with life on the dole when leaving school. The casual culture "came out" in the riots of 1981 when black and white youths burned and looted record shops and clothes shops and fought with the police. But the riots were just the moments when the pressure got too great and the lid blew off. There were other things bubbling away underneath all the violence – more positive things that didn't get noticed by the media and would never make it on to the television news.

Breaking for the border: soul meets reggae over London

"See, we're living in a time of rock 'n' roll,
New wave, hip hop and classical.

Come on everybody, turn the dial…"
(The World's Famous Supreme Team)

"From Brixton or whether Tottenham you have fe tune in to this yah rebel station.
(Dread Broadcasting Corporation [DBC]*)*

"Our aim is to free up the airwaves."*(Papa Lepke* [DBC]*)*

The first thing to go was the line between soul and reggae. We saw how that line had been broached with Lovers' rock in the late 1970s. And it was blurred even further in the next few years. In 1980, a soul band called Light of the World from East London recorded a funk version of *I shot the sheriff*. Soul bands (like Cashmere) began wearing dreadlocks. And the Mastermind Road Show, Britain's top eight man MC-dj hip hop team, came from Harlesden and had grown out of a reggae sound system. Flashing back and forth across six turntables, the Roadshow stuns the crowds with displays of homegrown British rap and dance which match the American originals. From the late 1970s onwards all-day discos began to mix soul and reggae under one roof.

With the advent of the twelve-inch record in the late 1970s soul began to follow the format established in reggae. On a twelve-inch soul record now the original cut with vocals (what used to be called the "A" side) will sit next to a "dub" version of the same melody/rhythm. On the other side of the record there may be other "dub" or "club" mixes of the same track. Sometimes different producers and engineers will be invited to preside over a "guest" mix, offering their own versions of the song. The record is held together round a rhythm but within this rhythm there is plenty of scope for improvisation. If rap helped to tighten and lighten up reggae, then it's also true that reggae has helped to unravel soul.

The pirate radio stations played a major role in this blurring of the two musics. Independent local radio had been set up in 1973 and by the early 1980s, forty-six licensed stations were operating in the UK. But neither these nor BBC's Radio One devoted much air-time to black music. In the capital, there was Steve Barnard's *Reggae Time* on Radio London (later taken over by Tony Williams). And from 1979 onwards, you could catch three-and-a-half hours of the hardest roots reggae going on David Rodigan's *Roots Rockers* show on Capitol. Soul fans got slightly better treatment. But the newer soul and hip hop didn't get much air-time at all.

Around 1983, off-shore pirate radio stations like Radio Laser and Radio Caroline began transmitting more black music in stereo from ships anchored in the North Sea. But the real breakthrough in radio piracy occurred when cheap portable transmitters came on the market. By the mid-1980s you could buy an (illegal) 50-watt radio transmitter for around £200 or build one yourself for less. Soul and reggae enthusiasts began to plug the gap in the airwaves playing solid funk, soul and dub. All they needed was a good quality cassette recorder, a transmitter and a high roof. Tower blocks provided the ideal transmission site. It's been estimated that a signal from a 40-watt transmitter broadcasting from the roof of a fifteen-storey tower block can reach a forty-mile radius. Tower blocks throughout Britain's cities sprouted aerials overnight. The pirates often pre-record their radio shows at home. They then walk into a block of flats and get up on the roof. Wearing soft shoes so as not to alert the people living in the flat below – trainers are perfect for this! – they creep across the roof, set up the transmitter and beam out the music of their choice to other enthusiasts. Meanwhile, if they lie down flat (not too near the edge), they can scan the horizon for radio detector vans and police cars. (The Home Office can track down the signal in about ten minutes, so the pirates have to be fast on their feet.)

Land-based pirate stations have mushroomed in Britain in the last few years. In May, 1985, John Hind and Stephen Mosco managed to locate 140 stations,[2] though not all of them broadcast music. And there were many more that they didn't manage to contact. In their list, London alone was host to sixty stations. Some of the stations grew into bigger and more permanent operations. Radio Invicta, the first land-based pirate, carried funk, electro funk, soul, gospel, jazz and r&b. And on Wednesday nights you could catch the Mastermind Roadshow crew doing high-speed cutting, scratching and mixing "live" on air. Another station, LWR (London Weekend Radio) became the home of hip hop. Tim Westwood, who pioneered LWR, brought the South Bronx to South London with his show. When Afrika Bambaata toured Britain in 1984 he used LWR to recruit members for the British chapter of the Zulu Nation. And the London hip hop tribe now gathers under the banner of Westwood's Westside Organisation, which is led by MC Spyrock. Westwood also organised a hip hop festival sponsored by the now de-funkt Greater London Council in 1984 at the South Bank complex. The display of dancing, mixing, graffiti and rap attracted over 30,000 people. Other stations like JFM (Jackie FM) and Horizon began broadcasting soul and jazz-funk.

Meanwhile in West London, DBC (Dread Broadcasting Corporation), founded by Papa Lepke, began pushing out highpowered reggae on Friday nights. The DBC format was based on sound system style and Mikey Dread's *Dread at the Controls* show on Jamaican radio. (This was taken off air in the post-Seaga clampdown.) Heavy dub echo and reverb were used in the links and the dj posse included Lepke's sister, Miss P and Papa Meka, a thirteen-year-old with a wild line in rootsy patter. Though reggae was the mainstay of DBC, the station also broadcast funk, r&b, Afrikan (South African black music) and soca (upbeat calypso). DBC was unique in Britain. A black-run station broadcasting black music to a mixed race audience. In the words of Miss P (who later went on to dj the first reggae show on BBC Radio One):

> "There's never been a station run like DBC. Our format allows us to play music that would otherwise never be heard publicly. We create movement within the industry. It's not that we want to create something that's strictly for blacks. The point is to show that a black person can actually get up and own and control something and employ white people, the same as we work. Then you have a good mixture and it shows we can work together.[3]

The pirate boom was checked by tighter legislation (the Tele-communications Act became law in 1984). Tougher fines and regular police raids, together with the dirty tactics adopted by some of the newer pirates to crowd out their rivals, pruned down the number of stations. But the pirates had provided a soundtrack for Britain's city-based youth to match the casual image. They had given people access to black music on a scale unprecedented in Britain since the earlier wave of off-shore pirates in the 1960s. And radio had all kinds of advantages over clubs. There are no age or dress restrictions with a radio. You don't have to get past burly bouncers to get to the music. All you have to do is switch the radio on and turn the dial. And you don't have to stay in one place all the time. You can travel up and down the wavelengths from Cape Town to the Caribbean via Brooklyn and Clapham Junction. If you own a radio-cassette recorder combination all you have to do is push the red button (James Brown's "peace button") and you can have a permanent record of your journey...

Conclusion: when the roots come home to roost

> "I was born in Britain, and as I never even visited Jamaica until 1971, my musical roots, if you like, were records we'd bring into the school lunch-time disco sessions... So my earliest roots were split between a lot of rock, some reggae, and the pentecostal gospel music I played guitar for in a

church up Kensal Rise [North West London]. Later on, of
course, I got heavily into jazz... What *is* roots? Music is
shapeless, colourless..."

(George Oban, formerly of Aswad*)*

In Bristol in South West England a hip hop dj called Milo (the
Bassmonger) is now scratching break-beats into reggae rhythms at
clubs and parties... In the early 1980s, Sly Dunbar and Robbie
Shakespeare, the drums and bass team responsible for the rockers
and rub-a-dub style rhythms that dominated Jamaican reggae for
almost a decade, work as sessions-men on the spacey disco funk
recordings of Jamaican New York singer, Grace Jones... And
Yellowman makes a toast-rapping record with Afrika Bambaata...
At the Wembley Arena in July, 1986, the Real Roxanne and Roxanne
Shanté, both from New York City, challenge each other to a rapping
duel to establish which one is the REALLY real Roxanne (the contest
remains undecided: New York City is chockablock with contenders
for the title)... In the same weekend, Dennis Brown plays a concert
in Finsbury Park, North London, in a line-up that also includes Latin
bands... In July again, Ruben Blades and Celia Cruz, king and
queen of salsa, tour Britain separately, playing to capacity crowds...
If you've got a radio, a record player or a tape deck you can listen to
the still popular Studio One ridims of the 1960s and the 1970s or to
the Rasta-Marxist calypsonian Black Stalin announcing that *Kaiso
Gone Dread*... If that doesn't suit your mood you can always tune in
to the apolitical soca of Lord Shorty or the Mighty Arrow (soca is
calypso filtered through disco, salsa, rock and jazz)... The
"progression" from the "simple" to the "complex", from vocal
chords and palms on drumskins to drum machines and electro
rhythms is turned round wild-style by people like Doug E. Fresh, the
Human Beat Box. Fresh uses his voice to impersonate the beat box
live on record... The roots are getting tangled up right now but the
vital mix is stronger than ever.

And where – in the end – are *my* roots? I'm a white Englishman
(whatever that is). I have no idea where my family came from
originally – the line gets wavy just two generations back. Someone
once told me that the name Hebdige comes from "the Baltic Plains"
and that's it. That's all I know. I once tried out the Baltic Plains
connection on a professor at an interview, hoping, I think, to impress
him. He looked thoughtful for a moment then told me that as far as he
knew there were no plains in the Baltic, under them or anywhere in
the immediate vicinity. I decided to renounce my Baltic ancestry
(perhaps I got it wrong, perhaps it was the *Balkan* plains...). If I have
any roots at all then they have been made in my own life-time, in my

own life. It's always been a case of cut 'n' mix. What else is there? Morris dancing? Baltic sea shanties?

In the local pub in July, 1986, I try out my current theory on what Caribbean music is on the young reggae MC who works at the mike on a Wednesday night. He doesn't look convinced. I've got it wrong again. The burn is on now in JA not GB, he tells me. *That's* where the sound is *really* moving right now. He reels off the names of toasters I've never heard of. When I get home I scribble them down: Admiral Bailey, Chakademus, Little Twitch... Maybe he's right. Who knows? One thing's for certain. He knows more about what's happening in reggae today than I do. I'm not even sure I got the names right...

Nobody can own a sound. Nobody can pin it down or put a copyright on it. It's better not to try.

But what's clear as daylight in Britain at the moment is that the chickens are coming home to roost. The British Empire has folded in upon itself. And as the pressure in the cities has mounted, the old national culture and national identity have started cracking at the seams. More and more people are growing up feeling, to use Colin MacInnes' phrase, "english half-english". There is an army of in-betweens and neither-nors out there who feel they belong to no given community. They realise that any community they might belong to in the future will have to be *made by them* or it won't get made at all. In some parts of Britain, West Indian patois has become *the* public language of inner-city youths, irrespective of their racial origin. When I interviewed a crew of (one white, two black) teenaged B-boys from Walsall in the West Midlands in 1984, they used three separate common languages. They talked to me in the local "Black Country" dialect. They joked and teased each other in Jamaican patois. And when describing their dance moves, they used the specialised South Bronx jargon of hip hop. Perhaps there is another nation being formed for the future beyond the boundaries of race. If that nation can't yet be visualised, then it can perhaps be heard in the rhythms of the airwaves, in the beat that binds together histories, cultures, new identities. The future is as blurred and as uncertain as the roots. It is as shapeless and as colourless as music itself.

Jo-Jo, a white reggae fan, interviewed in Birmingham's Balsall Heath, one of the oldest areas of black settlement in Britain, told Simon Jones recently:

"... there's no such thing as 'England' any more... welcome to India brothers! This is the Caribbean!...

Nigeria!... There is no England, man. This is what is coming. Balsall Heath is the centre of the melting pot, 'cos all I ever see when I go out is half-Arab, half-Pakistani, half-Jamaican, half-Scottish, half-Irish. I know 'cos I am [half Scottish/half Irish]... who am I?... Tell me who do I belong to? They criticise me, the good old England. Alright, where do I belong? You know I was brought up with blacks, Pakistanis, Africans, Asians, everything, you name it... who do I belong to?... I'm just a broad person. The earth is mine... you know we was not born in Jamaica... we was not born in 'England'. We were born here, man. It's our right. That's the way I see it. That's the way I deal with it."[4]

I can't top that. I won't even try.

Notes and References

PRE-MIX: VERSION TO VERSION
1. Albert Goldman, *Elvis*, Penguin, 1982.
2. Ibid.
3. Ibid.

ORIGINAL CUT – REBEL SOUND: REGGAE AND OTHER CARIBBEAN MUSIC

Chapter One: Slavery Days
1. See Richard Sheridan, *Sugar and Slavery: An Economic History of the British West Indies 1623–1775*, Caribbean University Press, 1974.
2. S. Davis and P. Simon, *Reggae Bloodlines*, Anchor, 1977.
3. Alex Haley, *Roots*, Picador, 1978.

Chapter Two: West African roots, West Indian flowers
1. David Simmons, *Black Rhythm and Roots*, BBC Radio Four, 1978.
2. J. L. Collier, *The Making of Jazz*, Granada, 1978.
3. David Simmons, op. cit., 1978.
4. Tony Harrison, "The Shakey Fairy", in *London Magazine*, April, 1970.
5. Machito interviewed by Stan Wooley in *Jazz Journal and Jazz Blues*, November, 1977.

Chapter Three: The music of Trinidad
1. See Andrew Carr, "The Calypso – a people's poetic platform: 'Massa, can you tel me what is dat thing?'" in *West Indian World* no. 215, 29 August–4 September, 1975; Mackie Burnette, "Pan and Caribbean Drum Rhythms" in *Jamaica Journal* vol. 11, nos. 3 and 4, March, 1978; C. R. Otley, *The Trinidad Callaloo: Life in Trinidad From 1851–1900*, Crusoe, 1978.

Chapter Four: Reggae and other Caribbean music
1. Cat Coore interviewed by Chris May in an article entitled "Third World-Roots Revolution", *Black Music*, January, 1979.

Chapter Five: The roots of reggae: religion and religious music
1. Gary Wills, "Martin Luther King is still on the case" in T. Wolfe (ed.), *New Journalism*, Picador, 1969.
2. Toots Hibbert quoted in S. Davis, op. cit., 1977.

Chapter Six: The Rastafarians
1. John Plummer, *Movement of Jah People*, Press Gang, 1978.
2. Ibid.
3. Joe Owens interviewed in "Rastas and Rude Boys", Programme 2 of 3 for BBC Radio and Open University, *Mass Communication and Society* Course DE353. (dir) Vic Lockwood, (pres) Dick Hebdige. First broadcast 1977. Available on tape from Open University.
4. Michael Thomas, "The Wild Side of Paradise", in *Rolling Stone*, 9 July, 1973.
5. John Plummer, op. cit., 1978.
6. Ibid.

7. Verena Reckford, "Rastafarian Music – An Introductory Study", in *Jamaica Journal* vol. 11, nos. 1, 2. Quarterly of the Institute of Jamaica, August, 1977.
8. Ibid.
9. Ibid.
10. Rico Rodriguez interviewed by Carl Gayle in "The Man from Wareika", *Black Music*, May, 1977.
11. Ibid.

Chapter Seven: The roots of reggae: black American music
1. Junior Lincoln interviewed in "Reggae – The Beginnings", Programme 1 of 3 for BBC Radio and Open University (see note 3, Chapter 6).
2. Lee Perry quoted in Chris May, "Starting from Scratch", *Black Music*, October, 1977.
3. Ibid.
4. S. Davis, op. cit., 1977.
5. Ibid.
6. Lee Perry quoted op. cit., October, 1977.
7. Ibid.
8. Joe Hill quoted in Chris May, "Cultural Reggae", *Black Music*, September, 1978.
9. Quoted in S. Davis, op. cit., 1977.

Chapter Eight: Rocksteady and the rude boy era
1. I Roy interviewed in "Rastas and Rude Boys", Programme 2 of 3 for BBC Radio and Open University (see note 3, Chapter 6).

Chapter Nine: Reggae
1. Lee Perry quoted in *Black Music*, October, 1977.
2. Ibid.
3. Niney quoted by Chris May in an article entitled "Blood and Fire" in *Black Music*, July, 1978.
4. Family Man quoted by Carl Gayle in an article entitled "Dread in a Babylon" in *Black Music*, September, 1975.
5. Big Youth quoted in S. Davis, op. cit., 1977.

Chapter Ten: Dub and talk over
1. Dermott Hussey quoted in "The Sound System" Programme 3 of 3 for BBC Radio and Open University (see note 3, Chapter 6).
2. S. Davis, op. cit., 1977.
3. Ibid.
4. *Black Music*, 1978.
5. I Roy interviewed in "Reggae – The Beginnings", Programme 1 of 3 for BBC Radio and Open University (see note 3, Chapter 6).
6. Ibid.
7. Chris May, "Sloley Does it", *Black Music*, September, 1978.

Chapter Eleven: Dread in a Inglan
1. Junior Lincoln in "The Sound System", Programme 3 of 3 for BBC Radio and Open University (see note 3, Chapter 6).
2. Count Shelley quoted in Chris May, "British Reggae 2", in *Black Music*, 1978. (This and the references cited in the following five notes together with those cited in notes 9 and 10 are only approximate. All the quotations come from a series of three articles on British reggae written by Chris May and published in the now defunct *Black Music* sometime between 1976 and 1978. I apologise for the imprecision but the intervening years – between writing the *Original Cut* and getting it published – have played havoc with my filing system!)
3. Philroy Mathias quoted in Chris May, "British Reggae 3", in *Black Music*, 1978.

4. Quoted in Chris May, "British Reggae 2", in *Black Music*, 1978.
5. David Hinds quoted in Chris May, "British Reggae 1", in *Black Music*, 1978.
6. Matumbi quoted in "British Reggae 2", in *Black Music*, 1978.
7. The Phantom quoted in "British Reggae 1", in *Black Music*, 1978.
8. Linton Kwesi Johnson, "Five Nights of Bleeding", from *Dread Beat and Blood*, Bogle – L'Ouverture, 1976.
9. Linton Kwesi Johnson quoted in Chris May, "British Reggae 1", in *Black Music*, 1978.
10. Linton Kwesi Johnson, *It Dread in a Inglan* (for George Lindo), op. cit., 1976.

DUB VERSION – THE RISE AND FALL OF TWO TONE
Chapter Twelve: Ska tissue: the rise and fall of Two Tone

1. The first record (excluding their own output) which the Beat brought out on Go Feet was Cedric Myton's *Heart of the Congos*, previously available in Britain only as an import.
2. From *The Two Tone Book for Rude Boys* by Miles, Omnibus Press, 1981.
3. Ibid.
4. Formed in 1976, Rock Against Racism was set up by people working in and around the rock industry to combat racism.
5. A similar submerged politics operated within Two Tone on the gender front. The Body Snatchers was an all-girl ska/reggae band formed by Nicky Singer, the rhythm guitarist. Probably the most significant contribution in this respect was made by Pauline Black, vocalist, with The Selecter. Dressed in a sharp suit and a bluebeat hat, she looked as "rough and tough" as any rude boy and provided a role model which contrasted with the image of dignified but passive womanhood enshrined in roots reggae where Rastafarianism still holds patriarchial sway. Pauline Black broke with the stereotype presented by groups like Bob Marley's backing singers, the regal but ultra-feminine I-Threes.
6. From *The Beat Twist and Crawl* by Malu Halasa, Eel Pie Publishing, 1981.
7. "Leapers" – English subcultural slang for amphetamines.
8. Also known as *God Save the Queen*, 1977.
9. *Stand down Margaret*, The Beat, Arista, 1980.
10. Peter York, *Style Wars*, Sidgwick & Jackson, 1980.
11. Halasa, op. cit., 1981.
12. Miles, op. cit., 1981.

CLUB MIX – BREAKING FOR THE BORDER
Chapter Thirteen: Sister Posse forward: is this the future?

1. See Amanda Lipman, "Sistas talk culcha", in *Spare Rib* no 160, November, 1985.

Chapter Fourteen: Slack style and Seaga

1. See S. Davis and P. Simon, *Reggae International*, Thames & Hudson, 1983, for an accessible account of the post-Seaga Jamaican political scene. The book also includes a foreword by Michael Manley and an interview with Edward Seaga.

Chapter Fifteen: Lover's rock: reggae, soul and broken hearts

1. See Sheryl Garratt, "Lovers' Rock", in *THE FACE* no 59, March, 1985, and John Futrell, "Lovers' Rock", in *Black Echoes* 13, December, 1980.
2. Clem Bushay quoted in *Black Echoes* 13, December, 1980.
3. Jackie of Alpha quoted in *Black Echoes* 13, December, 1980.

Chapter Sixteen: Rap and hip hop: the New York connection

1. Afrika Bambaata quoted in Steven Hager, "Afrika Bambaata's Hip Hop", in *Voice*, 21 September, 1982.
2. Grandmaster Flash quoted in Steven Harvey, "Spin Art", in *New York Rocker*, January, 1982.

3. Grandmaster Flash and The Furious Five quoted in Hager, op. cit., September, 1982.
4. See Mr Fresh and The Supreme Rockers, *Breakdancing*, Corgi, 1982.
5. James Brown quoted in David Toop, *The Rap Attack: African Jive to New York Hip Hop*, Pluto Press, 1984.
6. Malcom McLaren quoted in Hager, September, 1982.
7. Jerry Dammers quoted in Miles, *The Two-Tone Book for Rude Boys*, Omnibus, 1981.
8. Horace Gentleman, quoted ibid.
9. See Jeremy Marre and Hannah Charlton, *Beats of the Heart-Popular Music of the World*, Pluto Press, 1985.
10. Charlie Gillett, *Sound of the City*.
11. David Toop, op. cit., 1984.

Chapter Seventeen: Fast style reggae: designer label roots

1. See Sheryl Garratt, "Fast Forward", in *City Limits*, 24–30 August, 1984; Robert Elms, "Cultural Junction", in *THE FACE*, February, 1985.
2. See John Hind and Stephen Mosco, *Rebel Radio*, Pluto Press, 1985.
3. Miss P, quoted in Hind and Mosco, op. cit., 1985.
4. Simon Jones, *White Youth and Jamaican Popular Culture*, PhD thesis submitted at University of Birmingham, Centre for Contemporary Cultural Studies, 1986. An abridged version of this well researched and highly suggestive thesis which mixes together surveys of the literature on race, culture and popular music with an ethnography of white-black culture contact in the Birmingham area is to be published soon by Macmillan. Look out for it!

General index

saxa 57
Saxon International System 149, 152, 153
scratching 10, 138, 142, 145, 155, 157
scratch video 145
Seaga, Edward 22, 67, 122, 124, 125, 127, 155, 162
77 Club, 91
Shades (club) 114
Shabazz, Mrs Betty 145
shango 31, 32, 36, 39, 53
Sharpe, Sam 25, 47
Sheridan, Richard 160
shuffle 62, 65, 97, 146, 147, 148
signifying (word game) 147
Simmons, David 160
Simon, Peter 160
Sir Coxsone International System (UK) 129
Ska Bar, The (Club) 93
ska music 45, 58–60, 62–4, 70, 71, 72, 73, 75, 79, 83, 91, 97–8, 106–114, 127; origins of 127; rhythm defined 70; roots in rastafarian music 58–61; in US music 62–4; UK ska revival 97–8, 106–14
skinheads 93, 97, 106; revival 97
skip rope rhymes 147
slack mouth reggae 122–7, 135
slavery 22, 23–8, 47
soca music 16, 156, 157
soul music 28, 39, 46, 83, 98, 99, 128, 129, 131, 135, 153, 154, 155,
sound systems 62–68, 72–3, 87–9, 90, 91, 93, 94, 101, 112, 119, 125, 129, 137, 151–63, 155, 158; contests 63–4, 88, 92; early days in Jamaica 62–8; in New York 137; in UK 91–93, 94, 101, 112, 119, 125, 129, 137, 151–2, 155, 158; women in 119, 152, 153
spaghetti westerns 126, 144
specials (records) 83, 107
steel bands 20, 22, 35, 37–8, 39, 43, 56, 63, 91
steppers 45, 87, 153
stick fighting 36, 37, 38
Studio One 8, 75, 93, 157
sugar trade 23–4
Sugar Hill Records 147
Sunset Club, 91

Suspected Persons Act (sus) 100
swing 128
synthethiser 143

talk over 63–5, 82–9, 119–20, 125–7, 135, 146–7
tambour-bamboo bands 36, 37
Tamla Motown Records 135
Telecommunications Act, The 156
Thatcher, Margaret 111, 153
Third World Records (record store) 94
Thomas, Michael 21, 54, 160
Tin Pan Alley 132
Tommy Boy Records 145
toasting *see* talkover
Toop, David 163
Trinidad 34, 35–42, 56, 91
Top of the Pops (TV show) 80, 108
Trojan Records 92, 93, 97, 131
trumping in the spirit 50, 67, 84
Two Tone 98, 106–14, 162; movement contrasted with punk 110–1,

umbanda 31
Universal Negro Improvement Association (UNIA) 51, 53
uprock 140

Venture Records 94, 97
version, versioning 12–6, 83, 87, 88, 141
Virgin Records 45, 96, 97
voodoo 31, 32
vout 125

Waldorf, Stephen 119
Wavoka 106
West Indian Records 124
Westside Organisation 155
West Side Story (film) 111
wild style grafitti 136, 141, 155
Wild Style (film) 137
Williams, Dr Eric 43
Wills, Gary 9, 47
Wooley, Stan 160

York, Peter 111, 162

zulu music 145
Zulu Nation, The 139, 155

Index of musicians, singers, disc jockeys, record producers and sound system operators

Index to song and record titles